Constantius III

Constantius III

Rome's Lost Hope

Ian Hughes

Pen & Sword
MILITARY

First published in Great Britain in 2021 by
Pen & Sword Military
An imprint of
Pen & Sword Books Ltd
Yorkshire – Philadelphia

ISBN 978 1 52670 024 7

A CIP catalogue record for this book is
available from the British Library.

Typeset by Mac Style
Printed and bound in the UK by CPI Group (UK) Ltd,
Croydon, CR0 4YY

Pen & Sword Books Limited incorporates the imprints of Atlas,
Archaeology, Aviation, Discovery, Family History, Fiction, History,
Maritime, Military, Military Classics, Politics, Select, Transport,
True Crime, Air World, Frontline Publishing, Leo Cooper, Remember
When, Seaforth Publishing, The Praetorian Press, Wharncliffe
Local History, Wharncliffe Transport, Wharncliffe True Crime
and White Owl.

For a complete list of Pen & Sword titles please contact

PEN & SWORD BOOKS LIMITED
47 Church Street, Barnsley, South Yorkshire, S70 2AS, England
E-mail: enquiries@pen-and-sword.co.uk
Website: www.pen-and-sword.co.uk

Or

PEN AND SWORD BOOKS
1950 Lawrence Rd, Havertown, PA 19083, USA
E-mail: Uspen-and-sword@casematepublishers.com
Website: www.penandswordbooks.com

Contents

List of Maps

List of Plates

Acknowledgements

In my last book, due to restrictions of time and health issues and relief at completing the text, I completely forgot to include an Acknowledgements page, for which I have been rightly berated and rebuked by Joanna and Owen. Although this apology will not make up for the omission, I am hoping that it will at least help to reduce the volume of complaints I still receive for not recognizing their patience and support as I wrote a book on 'some Roman bloke'. Given that this is yet *another* book on a Roman, all I can say is that without them, this book would not have been completed.

Having said that, they may be relieved to know that this is the last book on fifth-century Rome. On the 'barbarian' side, *Gaiseric: The Vandal Who Sacked Rome*[1] runs from the accession of Gaiseric in 428 until his death in 477, while *Attila the Hun: Arch-Enemy of Rome*[2] tells the story of Attila from his accession in 434 to his death in 454.

On the Roman side, *Stilicho: The Vandal Who Saved Rome*,[3] covered the period from 395 to 408; *Aetius: Attila's Nemesis*[4] begins in 423 and ends in 454; and *Patricians and Emperors: The Last Rulers of the Western Roman Empire*[5] takes up the story in 454 and runs until the deposition/death of the last Roman emperor, either Romulus Augustulus in 476 (deposed) or Julius Nepos in 480, depending upon taste. This book covers the only gap in the Roman story, 408–423.

As usual, I would like to thank those who have made this book possible, especially my commissioning editor, Phil Sidnell, whose patience with me over the last few years of delays due to health problems and, during the writing of this book, the world's descent into pandemic and 'lockdowns' has reduced some of the pressures that have been faced. Attempting to write a book while my son sat his 'mock exams' at the dining-room table could have been the pressure that tipped me over the edge!

I would also like to thank the readers of my previous books who have encouraged me to continue writing despite all the problems we have all faced. Their support has helped me to continue through the bad times.

This book is hereby dedicated to all of the people mentioned above. Thank you all!

Introduction

The life and times of Constantius III are often overlooked when it comes to the study of late antiquity. This appears to be largely due to the fact that, although he was vital in stopping and settling the Goths in Aquitania, the sources around his period of supremacy are inconsistent and contradictory and his actual 'rule' as emperor was only a few short months in 421. In contrast, although they were never emperors, the supremacies of his predecessor Stilicho (395–408) and successor Aetius (423, 433–455) were both much longer and better-recorded. In addition, they both had supporters who wrote panegyrics which have survived; no such work exists for Constantius.

Constantius was born in Naissus at an unknown date. It is difficult to assess his date of birth as absolutely no mention is made in any of the sources as to his age at any point. However, as his predecessor Stilicho was born around the year 360, it can probably be assumed that Constantius was born either around this time or slightly later. He was to marry Aelia Galla Placidia, the sister of the emperor Honorius, but the sources hint that Placidia was unhappy with the prospect. This could either be due simply to a lack of attraction or may instead be due to the possibility that, as Placidia was born around 390, Constantius was much older than her and therefore seen by her as being unsuitable, or she may simply have disliked him. Consequently, it is possible to date Constantius' birth to sometime between 360, if he was a contemporary of Stilicho and therefore seen by Placidia as being too old for her, and 385 if Placidia simply did not like him. Consequently, he was aged anywhere between his early 20s and his early 50s when he came to the notice of historians in 411.

There is only one possible description of Constantius:

In public processions Constantius was downcast and sullen, a man with bulging eyes, a long neck and a broad head, who always slumped over the neck of the horse he was riding, darting glances here and there out of the corners of his eyes, so that all saw in him 'a mien worthy of a tyrant', as the saying goes. But at banquets and parties he was so cheerful and affable that he even competed with the clowns who often played before his table.

Olympiodorus, fragment 23, trans. Blockley.

To some degree the specifically physical aspects of Constantius are borne out by his images on coins. He does indeed appear to have a long neck, with slightly bulging eyes. The 'mien worthy of a tyrant', with Constantius darting furtive glances around him, is nowhere else repeated, but in the circumstance of fifth-century Roman politics is understandable: he was to rise to a position of influence and power, and even become emperor, during a period in which ministers were to rise and fall at an alarming rate. Caution, and even paranoia, may have been the watchword for a successful career in politics at this time.

His life and times are rarely studied, except in connection with other events, especially the settlement of the Goths in Gaul in 418–19. As a consequence, his life is seen through the lens of historians whose interpretation of his deeds is coloured by the Gothic settlement, in itself seen as being a major factor in the dissolution of the West. In this book, the attempt will be made to assess Constantius' acts within the wider context of events prior to the settlement, as well as to analyze his other deeds, both before and after 419.

Despite the title of this book, one factor needs to be remembered at all times. The lack of information in the sources means that the book cannot be a biography in the modern sense. If the fragmentary nature of the sources and the lack of detailed information make it impossible to outline even a clear chronology of events, it is obvious that any attempt to reach conclusions concerning Constantius' personality or strategy – whether political or military – is doomed to failure. Instead, the book will venture to fill as many gaps as possible, create a chronology which incorporates all the evidence, and attempt to peel away the years to study Constantius as a man, insofar as this is possible. Scholars of this period will find much that they disagree with, but this cannot be avoided.

The Sources

The main causes of controversy revolve around the surviving sources that cover this period. The sources fall into four broad categories: Ecclesiastical Histories (which include the *Hagiographies*, Lives of the Saints), Secular Histories, Letters and Chronicles. In addition, there are panegyrics, the law codes of the *Codex Theodosianus* and the *Codex Justinianus* and the *Notitia Dignitatum* (List of Imperial Offices). There are also several smaller works which sometimes give relevant information, for which see the 'List of Abbreviations' that follows the Introduction. Unfortunately, their fragmentary nature and large number means that there are too many to analyze individually. Only a brief description of some of the major sources is given here.

Secular Histories

Gregory of Tours (see Renatus Profuturus Frigeridus)

Jordanes (fl. 550s) wrote two books. The *Romana* (*On Rome*) is a very brief epitome of events from the founding of Rome until 552. Due to the fact that it is extremely condensed, it can be useful but offers little that cannot be found elsewhere. Jordanes also wrote the *Getica* (*Origins and Deeds of the Goths*). This work is valuable in that it contains a lot of information that would otherwise be lost, especially those sections which demonstrate a Gothic viewpoint. Unfortunately, due to its bias towards the Goths, it must be used with caution.[1]

Procopius (c.500–c.554) wrote the *Wars of Justinian*. In these he describes the wars fought by the general Belisarius on behalf of the Eastern Emperor Justinian. Included are many asides and brief entries concerning the history of the West and of the Germanic peoples who had overrun the Western Empire. It is usually assumed to be reliable, but caution is needed where his work concerns events outside his own lifetime.

Renatus Profuturus Frigeridus (fl. fifth century) wrote a history that only survives in fragments. Fortunately, he was used as a source by **Gregory of Tours** for his book *Historia Francorum* (*History of the Franks*), from which many items of value can be gleaned. The accuracy of these fragments is in many cases unknown.

Salvian (fl. fifth century) wrote a work known as *De gubernatione Dei* (*On the Government of God*, also known as *De praesenti judicio*) in which he describes life in fifth-century Gaul and contrasts the 'wickedness' of the Romans with the 'virtues' of the barbarians. Although written with a specific purpose, it can be used with care to furnish relevant information about conditions in Gaul after the invasions of 406.

Zosimus (c.500) wrote the *Historia Nova* (*New History*) which covers the period from the mid-third century to 410. He appears to have used two main sources for his information. Eunapius was used for events to 404 and Olympiodorus was used for the years from c.407 to 410. Zosimus was a pagan, writing in Constantinople, who was determined to show that Christianity was the reason for the disasters suffered by the Empire. He closely follows Eunapius and Olympiodorus. He is not critical of his sources, so although his work is useful it needs a great deal of caution when it is being used.

Ecclesiastical Histories and Associated Works

Augustine (354–430) wrote many works, including *De civitate dei* (*The City of God*), which was written after the Gothic sack of Rome in 410. It includes information which is useful in reconstructing circumstances concerning events around the time of the sack, but the moralizing Christian nature of the work needs to be taken into account.

Hagiographies: several of the 'Lives of the Saints' contain information concerning the era during which Constantius was alive. However, the fact that these works are aimed almost exclusively at promoting the sanctity of the individual being described means that they are not subjective and so extreme caution is needed in these cases.

Socrates Scholasticus (born c.380) wrote the *Historia Ecclesiastica* (*Church History*) which covers the years 305 to 439. It was written during the reign of Emperor Theodosius II (408–450). Written solely as a history of the church, it contains much information on secular events, but mainly only where they impinge on church history. However, these items are otherwise unrecorded so they can offer unique insights.

Theoderet (c.393–c.457) wrote many works on Christian doctrine, but more importantly also wrote a *Historia Ecclesiastica* (*Church History*) which begins in 325 and ends in 429. He used several sources including, among others, Sozomen, Rufinus, Eusebius and Socrates. Possibly due to the mixed nature of his sources, the work is chronologically confused and must be used with caution.

Letters

Many letters written at this time survive. Although most are obviously of a personal nature, some include information on secular events and on some of the leading men of the time. These can be valuable in filling in details but their accuracy in most areas remains unknown.

Apart from his religious treatises, Augustine was a prolific writer of letters, many of which are still extant. They give an impression of what life was like in early fifth-century Africa, as well as occasionally giving useful information concerning secular events.

Sidonius Apollinaris is the most important source for conditions in Gaul during the last years of the West. His many letters illuminate relations between Goths and the Roman elite, as well as demonstrating the changing attitudes of the aristocracy towards their 'barbarian' overlords. However, at all times the biases of a Roman aristocrat need to be borne in mind, along with the position of the recipient of the letter: a letter to a fellow aristocrat may contain disparaging remarks about the Goths, whereas a letter to a Goth would certainly not contain these.

Chronicles[2]

The chronicle was the form of history which 'so well suited the taste of the new Christian culture that it became the most popular historical genre of the Middle Ages'.[3] The positive aspect of this popularity is that several chronicles have survived. The negative aspect is that they displaced conventional history as the means of transmitting information about the past and so no complete histories written during the fifth century survive.

There is a further feature that causes difficulty when analyzing the chronicles, especially the fragmentary ones. Several collections of these sources were made prior to the twentieth century. Each of these collections could give the sources different titles. For example, the works referenced as the *Anonymus Cuspiniani* in secondary sources from the early twentieth century and before are now referred to as the *Fasti Vindobonenses Priori*, following Mommsen's description in the *Chronica Minora*, Vol. 1 (see Bibliography). Therefore readers should be aware that references in this book are likely to differ from these earlier works.

The *Chronica Gallica of 452* is a continuation of the Chronicle of Jerome covering the years 379 to 452. The *Chronica Gallica of 511* also begins in 379 and continues to 511. Due to the similarity between the two, it is possible to see the Chronicle of 511 as a continuation of the Chronicle of 452. Both these works contain useful information, but need to be used with care since the dates given may not in fact be accurate. The *Gallic Chronicle of 452* only becomes accurate after 447, and here the events in Gaul are the most accurately dated. Prior to 447 the chronology is extremely confused.[4] The *Gallic Chronicle of 452* has some entries undated. In these the reference is simply to the modern 'number' given to the entry. For example, the invasion of Italy by Radagaisus is undated and is therefore referenced simply as 'no. 50'.

The *Chronicon Paschale* (Easter Chronicle, so-called because of the author's use of Easter as the focus of his dating system) is an anonymous chronicle dating from the early seventh century, compiled in Constantinople.[5] Although it is a later document and some of the dates and 'facts' are wrong, the *Chronicon Paschale* is useful in confirming other sources and adding detail to events. However, it must be used with caution thanks to the temporal distance between its compilation and the early fifth century.

Hydatius (c.400–c.469) lived in Hispania and wrote a continuation of the Chronicles of Eusebius and Jerome, beginning with the accession of Theodosius in 379 and finishing in 468, so he appears to have finished writing in 469. His work has serious errors in dating that are still confusing. These are probably caused by the fact that much of his information was late arriving in Hispania, being taken there by embassies and merchants whose dating was insecure.[6] For events in Spain his work is good and relatively accurate.[7] Although potentially valuable, the errors mean that Hydatius must be used with caution, with dates especially being confirmed by other sources whenever possible.

John Malalas (fl. sixth century) wrote a chronicle intended to be used by both churchmen and laymen. Unfortunately, the work covers 'history' from the biblical period to the reign of Justinian in one book, so much is glossed over or omitted. As a result, the work is useful in places but this is rare.

Marcellinus Comes (fl. sixth century) wrote a chronicle that covers the period from 379 to 534 (an unknown writer continued the chronicle down to 566). It is mainly concerned with the Eastern Empire, but includes some information concerning the West, drawn mainly from Orosius. Where possible this information needs to be confirmed by independent sources to ensure the accuracy of dates and the reliability of information contained.

Difficulties with the Chronicles

The modern concept of a chronicle is that events are accurately dated and each single occurrence is allocated a separate entry in its relevant date. This preconception has badly affected perceptions of the Chronicles, leading to accusations of inaccuracy and a poor grasp of time.

In fact, some of these observations are unfair to the chroniclers. Even in the modern era, in which access to periodicals, newspapers and the internet is common, one of the most common radio competitions is 'Guess the Year'. It is clear that without modern methods of establishing specific dates, such as newspaper archives, human error in reporting events is to be expected.

Furthermore, ancient chroniclers were not writing with modern expectations in mind. As long as events were in roughly the correct order, the chronicle would fulfil its purpose. Therefore it is a common occurrence for the chronicler to include later events at a convenient place earlier in his account.

For example, in the *Chronicon Paschale* in the entry dated to 437, where the chronicler describes the marriage of Valentinian III and Eudoxia, he notes: 'And he celebrated his nuptial, taking Eudoxia, the daughter of Theodosius and Eudocia Augusti, in the month Hyperberetaeus, on day four before Kalends of November, and by her he had two daughters, Eudocia and Placidia.' The entry highlights the fact that the chroniclers were including later events at convenient places within the earlier entries, unless Eudocia experienced two extremely fast gestation periods.

A further problem with the Chroniclers is that they use different methods for calculating dates. For example, Prosper and Hydatius use a different method of calculating Christ's passion, Prosper dating this to the fifteenth year of Tiberius, Hydatius to the start of Tiberius' fifteenth regnal year. This discrepancy helps to explain the differences in dates between the two chronicles.[8] The consular date used by Prosper, plus his closer proximity to events, results in his dating system being preferred on the majority of occasions.

Panegyrics

When reading panegyrics one piece of advice is worth remembering: 'Notoriously, however, the aim of the panegyrist is not to tell the truth, but to glorify his subject, exaggerating the good and suppressing or distorting the bad, the inappropriate, or the inconvenient.'[9] Where panegyrics are used, these will be assessed on an individual basis within the text.

Other Sources

The *Notitia Dignitatum*
This is an extremely important document. It purports to list the bureaucratic and military organization of both the Eastern and Western Empires. Thousands of offices are listed. Dated to c.395 for the East and c.420 for the West, it is potentially a mine of statistical and legal information. Unfortunately there are many problems. Probably originating with the Emperor Theodosius in the East, it may in theory have been intended as a full list of offices. The Eastern section of the *Notitia* appears to date from some time in the early 400s. As a result, it is usually believed that the surviving document is a copy preserved

in the West of the Eastern *Notitia* dating from the reign of Arcadius (395–408). Unfortunately, it was not kept strictly up to date and there are many omissions and duplications. Moreover, due to the fragmentation of the Empire during and immediately after Stilicho's death in 408, it is uncertain whether many of the army units listed existed in reality or only on paper. As a consequence, information taken from the *Notitia* should be accepted as possible rather than certain.

There appear to have been later attempts to update the Western portion of the document and evidence suggests that these were last compiled at some date in the 420s, possibly under the orders of Constantius. Consequently, in theory the document is of inestimable use for Constantius' mindset in 321. Unfortunately, there are internal problems with the *Notitia* which suggest that it does not reflect reality. For example, although the provinces of Britain had drifted out of the imperial orbit in the early 410s, the leaders and troops associated with the island are still included in the *Notitia*. The same is true of the provinces of Belgica and Germania. The fact that these are 'unquestionably anachronistic' suggests that the document includes material reflecting what had once been available to the Empire rather than the current military status.[10] Yet the document may also have been a statement of intent. If it was compiled under the orders of Constantius III in 421, it may have been his intention as emperor to restore the glory of the West and incorporate the lost provinces back into the Empire.

As well as being useful in outlining what the Roman bureaucracy believed should have been the case, it is also possible to analyze the document in the hope of gleaning material concerning the condition and deployment of the army. This is covered in more depth below.

The *Codex Theodosianus*

The *Codex Theodosianus* is a collection made during the reign of Theodosius II in the East of all the laws issued since the reign of Constantine I (306–337). Added to this body of laws were the new laws (*novellae*) passed by Theodosius II (*Nov. Th.*) and Valentinian (*Nov. Val.*) after 439. These were also collected and kept with the Codex, and now form part of the main text.

The 'Code' and the 'Novels' are a valuable source of material for the period. It is possible to analyze the laws to establish their context and so determine the reasons for their passing. Furthermore, the laws are accompanied by the names of the emperor(s) that passed them, in most cases by the precise date on which they were passed, and by the name of the city in which the emperor passed the law. This allows us to trace some of the movements of the emperor, and also enables us to link specific laws with specific events, although this evidence is often not wholly convincing.

It is also interesting to note that one of the laws dismisses laws that were destined to be 'valid for the cases of their own time only'.[11] This highlights the fact that, like modern law, some laws passed by emperors were meant to deal with specific emergencies and events. After these had passed, the laws were naturally allowed to lapse. Modern examples include the laws passed to deal with the 'emergency' that was the Second World War. Once this war was over, these laws were repealed and 'normality' resumed.

Conclusion

The information that is available in the sources should not detract us from the knowledge that they were all written with a purpose. Even when this bias is openly declared, it can easily be overlooked or forgotten. If this is the case with the major sources as listed above, it is even more the case with the multitude of minor sources not listed. The less important sources that are used are of varying accuracy and utility and where necessary an analysis of these will be dealt with in the body of the text. However, if the source only gives us one or two snippets of information, then it is possible that the source will not be analyzed.

One problem with all the sources needs to be highlighted. This is where the sources inform the reader of political intrigue. The difficulty lies with the fact that the sources claim to know details of the kind which are always most suspicious: 'tales of secret intrigues and treasons which could not be known to the world at large.'[12] Whenever this kind of information is encountered, a full analysis will be attempted to decide whether there is the possibility of the author knowing the full details of events.

Spelling and Terminology

Wherever possible the simplest definitions and spellings have been used throughout the book. There are many examples in the ancient sources of variations in the spelling of individuals' names.[13] Also, in most modern works Roman spellings are usually 'modernized' by removing the common 'us' endings and substituting a modern variant. Wherever possible, the most widely-used variant has been employed in the hope of avoiding confusion.

When describing both the tribes along the Rhine and those who successfully invaded the Empire, at times the phrase 'barbarian' rather than 'German' has been used. Although the word 'barbarian' is now out of fashion, largely due to its negative aspects regarding comparative civilization levels with the Romans, it has been used as it is an otherwise neutral term, whereas the use of the word 'German' often implies 'community and ethnicity on the basis of shared language' which is actually misleading.[14]

In most cases the term 'Goth/s' has been used rather than 'Visigoth/s'. Contemporary sources describe both the Visigoths and the Ostrogoths simply as 'Goths'.[15] During Constantius' lifetime there was only one 'Gothic' threat, and that was the Goths in the West. The Ostrogoths were peripheral, living in the faraway regions of Eastern Europe. It was only after their invasion of Italy under Theoderic in 493 that the West was forced to divide the terminology. Only where there may be confusion between the two 'tribes' will the terms 'Visigoth' and 'Ostrogoth' be used.

Abbreviations

In order to make the references more manageable, the following abbreviations have been used for ancient sources:

Additamenta Ad Chronicon Prosperi Hauniensis	*Addit. Ad Prosp. Haun.*
Agathias	Agath.
Ammianus Marcellinus	Amm. Marc.
Annales Ravennae	*Ann. Rav.*
Augustine	Aug.
Aurelius Victor	Aur. Vict.
Callisthenes	Call.
Cambridge Ancient History	CAH
Cassiodorus, Chronicle	Cass. Chron.
Chronica Gallica of 452	*Chron. Gall.* 452
Chronica Gallica of 511	*Chron. Gall.* 511
Chronica Minora (Mommsen)	*Chron. Min.*
Chronicon Paschale	*Chron. Pasch.*
Claudian Claudianus (Claudian)	Claud.
Codex Justinianus	*Cod. Just.*
Codex Theodosianus	*Cod. Th.*
Collectio Avellana	*Collect. Avell.*
Constantius of Lyon	Const.
Eunapius of Sardis	Eun.
Eutropius	Eut.
Evagrius	Evag.
Fasti vindobonenses posteriors	*Fast. Vind. Post.*
Fasti vindobonenses priores	*Fast. Vind. Prior.*
Gaudentius	Gaud.
Gildas	Gild.
Gregory of Tours	Greg. Tur.
Hydatius	Hyd.
John of Antioch	Joh. Ant.

John Malalas	Joh. Mal.
Jordanes	Jord.
Libanius	Lib.
Marcellinus Comes	Marc. Com.
Merobaudes	Merob.
Minutes of the Senate	Min. Sen.
Nestorius	Nest.
Nicephorus Callistus	Nic. Call.
Notitia Dignitatum	*Not. Dig.*
Novellae Theodosianae	*Nov. Theod.*
Novellae Valentinianae	*Nov. Val.*
Olympiodorus of Thebes	Olymp.
Orosius	Oros.
Paulinus of Nola	Paul.
Paulinus of Pella	Paul. Pell.
Paulus Diaconus	Paul. Diac.
Philostorgius	Philost.
Possidius	Poss.
Priscus, *Chronica*	Prisc. *Chron.*
Priscus, *Romana*	Prisc. *Rom.*
Procopius	Proc.
Prosopography of the Later Roman Empire	PLRE
Prosper Tiro	Prosp.
Pseudo-Augustine	Pseudo-Aug.
Renatus Profuturus Frigeridus	Ren. Prof.
Saint Jerome	Jer.
Salvian	Salv.
Scriptores Historiae Augustae	*Scrip. His.*
Sidonius Apollinaris	Sid. Ap.
Sirmondian Constitutions	*Sirm.*
Socrates Scholasticus	Soc.
Sozomen	Soz.
Suidas	Suid.
Theoderet	Theod.
Theophanes	Theoph.
Vegetius	Veg.
Victor of Vita	Vict. Vit.
Zosimus	Zos.

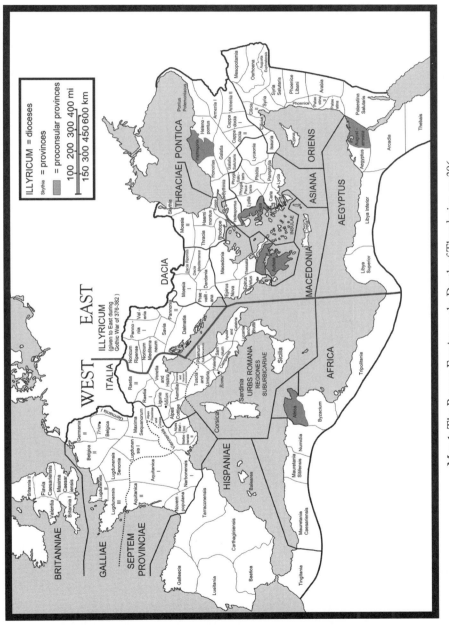

Map 1: The Roman Empire on the Death of Theodosius, AD 396.

Chapter One

Historical Background and Early Years

Historical Background

At the time of the birth of Constantius, sometime probably between 360 and 385, the Roman Empire had been in existence for several centuries. During that time the Empire had constantly evolved and during the reign of Diocletian had changed from what historians call the *Principate*, where the emperor was called *Princeps* ('First') and depicted as being simply the 'first among equals' (an illusion created by the first emperor Augustus in order to cement his position after years of civil war), to a period known as the *Dominate*, where the emperor was called *Dominus* ('Lord') and was seen as being exalted above all others.

In addition, the city of Rome was now only the nominal capital of the Roman Empire. Instead, several new cities had emerged as the major political centres of the Empire: for example, Trier and Milan in the West and Constantinople, Sirmium and Antioch in the East. In most cases this was in large part due to their strategic locations.

The End of the Fourth Century

In 324 Constantine became emperor of the whole Empire. His dynasty (the 'Flavian' or 'Constantinian') lasted until the death of Julian (r. 360–363) – known as 'The Apostate' because of his support for Paganism – who gathered his troops and led an ill-fated invasion of Persia, during the course of which he died.

A man named Jovian (363–364) was proclaimed emperor, but soon afterwards he too died. His successor was Valentinian (364–375) who, after being acclaimed by the army and close officials, quickly acclaimed his brother Valens (364–378) as co-*Augustus*, with Valentinian taking the West and Valens the East. From this point onwards, with few exceptions, the Empire was to be divided between (usually) two rulers, one in the East and one in the West.

After the death of Valentinian in 375 his sons Gratian and Valentinian II were acclaimed joint emperors in the West. In the East, where Valens remained emperor, in 376 a large band of Goths appeared on the banks of the Danube seeking sanctuary from the Huns. Valens allowed them entry to the Empire, but they were badly treated and broke into open revolt. In 378 Valens gathered an army together and led his forces to face the Goths in battle. Contrary to expectations, Valens was defeated and killed by the Goths at the Battle of Adrianople. Gratian in the West, the eldest son of Valentinian, was now the senior emperor. To rule the East Gratian chose Theodosius, the son of a man also called Theodosius who had displayed military ability in the West before being arrested and executed in 376.

With Theodosius in the East and Gratian and Valentinian II in the West, the Empire was slowly able to recover. After being defeated in a second battle against the Goths, Theodosius led his forces in a campaign aimed at restricting the Goths' access to supplies and, in 382, his strategy proved effective: the Goths capitulated. Although the Goths were 'beaten' and forced to accept a treaty, they had not been crushed and remained united under their own leaders; an unprecedented move and one that would have dire consequences for the West.

Theodosius and the Civil Wars

With imperial focus being on other events, imperial neglect of Britannia resulted in a man named Magnus Maximus being proclaimed as emperor by the British troops (r. 383–388). When Maximus crossed to Gaul, Gratian's troops deserted and Gratian was captured and executed. After a brief hiatus, Maximus invaded Italy to overthrow Valentinian II. This was unacceptable to the Eastern emperor Theodosius, who in 388 declared war and defeated Maximus at the Battle of the Save, inflicting heavy casualties on the Western army.

Theodosius now installed a Frankish general named Arbogast to support the young Western emperor Valentinian but, instead of the situation calming down, Valentinian died in mysterious circumstances. Shortly afterwards Arbogast proclaimed a man named Eugenius as Emperor of the West. Theodosius was outraged and in a repeat of earlier events, he invaded the West. At the Battle of the Frigidus in 394 he again heavily defeated the Western army, removing Eugenius and Arbogast from power. He then proclaimed his son Honorius as ruler in the West, with Stilicho, the husband of Theodosius' adopted daughter Serena, as regent. At this point the Western Empire was fully functional, with Britannia, Hispania and Gaul well within the imperial remit.[1]

Constantius

When Theodosius died unexpectedly in early 395, Constantius' age is unknown. Given that he would be mentioned in 411 as the West's supreme commander, it is likely that in 395 he was probably in his 20s, if not slightly older. If so, and given his later status, then it is likely that, being born in Naissus, he was part of the army that fought under Theodosius at the Battle of the Frigidus in 395. That he was later commander of the Western armies implies that, at the same time as Stilicho was named regent for Honorius, Constantius was one of the 'Eastern' military commanders appointed to join Stilicho in securing the West. If this is in any way accurate, then it is possible to further conclude that Constantius began his career in the elite corps of the *protectores*.

Why Constantius could have been earmarked for the *protectores* is completely unknown. The most likely reason is one of patronage. Constantius had been born in Naissus, as had so many of his predecessors in the army, including, for example, the Emperor Constantine. Consequently, it is highly likely that by the time of Constantius' maturity there was a network of soldiers within the higher ranks of the army who had been born in the region of Naissus and who promoted the sons and brothers of relatives and friends from the region. Given Constantius' name, it is even possible that he had some distant relationship to the Emperor Constantine I (whose father and son were also named Constantius), although this is nowhere indicated in the sources and his name may have been simply a coincidence. Whatever the case, it would appear that Constantius benefited from some form of patronage to arrive at a senior post within the army.

The *protectores* originated in the third century and over time became a bodyguard unit, reserved for individuals who were earmarked for rapid promotion. At an unknown time, and again like his older contemporary Stilicho, Constantius may have been transferred to the *Tribunus*

Praetorianus (*Partis Militaris*), ('Military Praetorian Tribune', a tribune and notary on the imperial general staff).[2] It is difficult to be exact about the nature of this post, mainly because very little information has survived in the sources. The little we know of the *Tribunus Praetorianus* suggests that it may have been an honorary title, 'the significance of which is not clear' but which is known to have come with several privileges.[3]

Although impossible to prove, it is here assumed that Constantius did indeed serve as a *Protector* and a *Tribunus Praetorianus* prior to his being posted to the West to serve as part of the military establishment under Stilicho. In this way he would be instantly eligible for promotion when events in the West required a new *magister militum*.

The Civil Service

The 'bureaucracy' of the Empire had earlier been divided between the military and the civil. Despite this separation, the civil service, or *militia officialis*, was always classed as part of the army, wearing military uniform, receiving rations, bearing the old 'non-commissioned' ranks of the army and being entered on the rolls of 'fictive' units. For example, all clerks of the praetorian prefecture were enrolled in *Legio I Adiutrix*, a unit that had long ago ceased to exist as a military formation.[4] The top civilian post was the *Praefectus Praetorio* (Praetorian Prefect). The prefects acted as the emperor's representative, governing in his name with legal, administrative and financial powers. Yet these were not the only powerful individuals at court.

The earlier *consistorium* (Consistory or council) had consisted of any individual ministers that the emperor wanted to consult about a specific topic. By this later date the *consistorium* had become more of a formal body with specific duties.[5] Its place as a 'council of specialists' was taken by the *proceres palatii* (Notables of the Palace), sometimes simply known as the *palatium* (palace). As its name implies, this was formed largely from those individuals whose employment kept them in close proximity to the emperor. Closest to the emperor, at least physically, was his personal household. Included in this category were the *protectores et domestici* (corps of officer cadets). If the postulations above are correct, Constantius was at the heart of the imperial court.

Of more importance were the principal imperial ministers, whose support and advice would be of great consequence to the emperor. Among the most powerful of these men were the *magister officiorum* (Master of Offices) and the *Comes sacrarum largitionum* (Count of the Sacred Largesses). The *magister officiorum* had many duties, including command of the *agentes in rebus* (imperial couriers) and control of the *scholae* (imperial bodyguard). He also controlled the *officia dispositionum* and *admissionum*, and so managed the emperor's timetable and audiences. The *Comes sacrarum largitionum* was in charge of finances, controlling the precious metal mines, the mints, and all revenue and expenditure in coin.[6] These individuals each commanded a large number of men who served as *rei privatae* (Private Secretaries). They tended to be fiercely competitive and protective of their powers, rights and privileges, and friction between the top ministers was endemic.

All or any of these men could expect to be consulted by the emperor on important issues concerning their special field, and in the case of the most powerful individuals with regard to the whole running of the Empire. Yet the delineation between these posts, especially at the top, was relatively narrow, and as a result often overlapped. This tended to exacerbate the friction between the top ministers of the Empire.[7] Stilicho, Constantius' superior officer, would soon find himself at the wrong end of these competitive frictions.

The Army

The Civil Service accounted for only a tiny fraction of the population of the Empire, and a career in it appears to have been seen as a means of self-promotion and security. The same cannot be said of the army. The army was restructured at the same time as the Civil Service. Although sometimes perceived as a precursor to modern military hierarchies, care must be taken when looking at the organization and apparent modernity that is usually represented.

This is nowhere borne out more than in the *Notitia Dignitatum*.[8] This massive document lists the post-holders of the Roman army in a very hierarchical structure, with lower ranks apparently responsible to their superior. Although this is a very easy assumption to make, in reality things were not necessarily as they appear.

In theory, the emperor was the undisputed head of the armed forces. However, as events in the third century had shown that the emperor could not be at all points where danger threatened, from the reign of Valentinian and Valens the Empire was permanently ruled by two different emperors at separate courts in the East and West. In the West, as time passed, the command of the army moved away from the emperor and devolved upon the newly-created *magister peditum* (Master of the Infantry) and *magister equitum* (Master of the Cavalry). In the course of time the *magister peditum* became the more senior of the two posts. Yet in the fifth century the Western *magister peditum* had a major problem: the series of civil wars fought by Theodosius I at the end of the fourth century had greatly weakened the Western army. Coupled with the loss of the Illyrian recruiting grounds to the East after the Battle of Adrianople, Stilicho, Constantius III and their successors would always be short of the manpower necessary to fully re-establish the borders of the West.

Finance and Taxation

In the fifth century inflation was still rampant in the West, despite the reforms of Diocletian (284–305) and Constantine I (306–337) and other attempts to calm matters by later emperors. Although these had resulted in the stabilization of the 'gold' economy, lower denomination coins continued to be debased. Furthermore, the coins for the West were being produced by only six official mints: Trier, Lyon and Arles in Gaul, Sirmium in Pannonia, plus Aquileia and Rome in Italy.

In earlier centuries coins had been common items, their distribution largely being initiated by payments to the army, from where they had spread throughout the local economy. However, the cost of the army had taken its toll and in this later period there is some evidence of units not being paid. During the late fourth century the troops began to be paid in kind (supplies of food, etc.) rather than in coin.[9] The change from a monetary system to one based upon agricultural production would have aggravated the pre-existing economic instability and so ensured that many individuals became disenchanted with Roman rule.

To further exacerbate feelings of unhappiness, many of the larger landowners – including some of the richest people in the Empire – were exempt from the payment of many of the taxes. It would have been galling to the poorer members of society to note that the rich avoided having to pay taxes. Even where they had to pay, the taxes were not 'progressive' – i.e. the rich paid the same amount of tax as the poor – leading to a further increase in the sense of disenfranchisement among the poor and middle classes.

Yet despite these difficulties the Empire continued to survive. This was thanks largely to the fact that a proportion of the state's income came from 'public lands'. These lands, either deserted thanks to the passage of war or confiscated from 'traitors' or from pagan temples by Christian emperors or lying intestate or unexploited, were appropriated by the state and leased out by bailiffs to peasants, so ensuring a slow, steady trickle of money into the imperial coffers.[10]

This money was supplemented by taxes on mines, quarries and on the mints themselves, but these provided only a limited amount of revenue. As a result, the Empire was forced to rely on the taxation of the poor and the middle classes, and only attempted to coerce the senatorial aristocracy to provide funds in times of dire emergency, a move which was always resented and resisted by the aristocracy.

The Citizens

It is possible to see the later Empire as one in which the divisions within society contributed to the fall of the West. Over time the rich became wealthier. This was partly because many farmers were forced to sell their lands or their service to the rich to fulfil their tax obligations. Consequently, the rich greatly increased their holdings and wealth while many of the poorer people were forced into poverty. Many of the poor entered a patron-client arrangement with local political or military officials. The officials came to be given the name *potentes* to distinguish them from their clients. The net result of these developments was the creation of a 'submerged economy' and 'the formation of social groups no longer in contact with the state'.[11]

In those areas where the more powerful individuals also lost faith in the Empire, or where service was deemed worthless, the rich could turn to the Church. This is the period during which the Church cemented its position of authority and also copied the administrative structure of the Empire, an organization that exists to this day. The civilian bureaucracy (*militia officialis*) and the army (*militia armata*) were joined by the 'Soldiers of Christ' (*militia Christi*).[12] Although this helped the

Church to prosper and grow, the result was a loss of manpower to both the bureaucratic and military arms of the Empire. Individuals wishing to evade their responsibility as 'functionaries of the State' instead joined the clergy, sometimes as bishops and men of great ecclesiastical and political power, but where this was not available simply as monks.[13]

There are two main outcomes of these changes. One was that the wealthy came to hold power greatly disproportionate to their numbers. Once ensconced in their position, these same men tended to use their influence to protect their own interests rather than that of the state. An example of their influence may be seen in the repeated elevation of usurpers in outlying provinces to the role of 'emperor'.

Apart from taxation, the main cause of unrest may have been the laws that tied people to their place of residence and to their jobs.[14] In Gaul there was another reason for dissatisfaction. In the early fifth century the headquarters of the Praetorian Prefect of Gaul moved from Trier in the north to Arles in the south. The move alienated a large part of northern Gaul and all of Britannia, since it reinforced the concept that the emperor and his court were more concerned with the core of the Empire and that those provinces on the northern periphery would, as a consequence, be neglected.[15] Furthermore, the emperor moved his court from Milan, where it was easily accessible, to Ravenna, where access from northern Gaul and Britannia was poor. The move helped to alienate the indigenous aristocracy of the north-west of the Empire, who were already tempted to join the Church rather than serve the Empire.

Linked to these changes is the fact that over a long period of time there was a transfer of loyalty. In the earlier Empire the bonds of loyalty had run from the poor, to the wealthy, to the aristocracy, and finally to the emperor. In the late third and early fourth century many of the wealthy and the aristocracy entered the Church. The bonds then ran from the poor, to the wealthy, to the Church. The emperor was eliminated from the equation and loyalties reverted from the abstract 'Empire' to the more concrete person of the local bishop. Over time, the Church replaced the Empire as the focus of people's lives.

In the outer regions, the result of these unpopular laws, the civil wars, the movement of political centres and the barbarian invasions was a tendency for the poor and unprotected to begin to 'cluster' more tightly to the heads of their families and they in turn to their aristocratic master or to the local warlord.[16] This may have been the cause of at least some of the 'uprisings' given the title *Bacaudic*. The origin and nature of the *bacaudae* remains unclear, but it would seem that when it began the phenomenon was mainly one of armed 'uprisings' by peasants in the less Romanized areas of Gaul and Spain. The movement may have been enlarged, if not started, as a result of poorer peasants taking up arms to protect themselves and/or survive. The first recorded uprising under the name *bacaudae* was c.283–84, when Gallic peasants rebelled against their treatment.[17] By the fifth century the word *bacaudae* was being used as a generic term for any uprising against the Empire where the leader did not aim at becoming emperor, or where the local aristocrats or middle classes refused to accept their subservience to Rome, preferring the protection of a local warlord.[18]

As the Empire slowly began to withdraw its influence from the northern borders, the Germanic tribes slowly began to increase theirs. The Franks, for example, were beginning the gradual widening of their influence over northern Gaul. Yet for the most part this was a very gradual process and the full effects would not be felt until sometime in the future.

Conclusion

The late fourth and early fifth century saw the Western Empire come under increasing pressure from two main sources. One was the risk of usurpations within the Empire thanks to the raising of taxes to fund protection for citizens which they did not then receive, which caused people to seek local protection rather than rely upon the invisible presence of the imperial legions. The second was that barbarians, both inside and outside the Empire, no longer took part in raids simply for financial gain. Instead, their leaders were intent on gaining land and prestige within the Empire, and their followers wanted to find land to settle which was free from the threat of either the Huns or other expanding 'barbarian' tribes, possibly following the example set by the Goths after the treaty of 382. These two factors would be the main causes of the slow death of the Western Empire.

However, at the turn of the fifth century the concept that the Empire would fall had not entered the minds of the majority of Roman citizens: the Empire had been around for centuries and would be around for centuries more. Then a series of events after the death of Theodosius threw the Western Empire into turmoil.

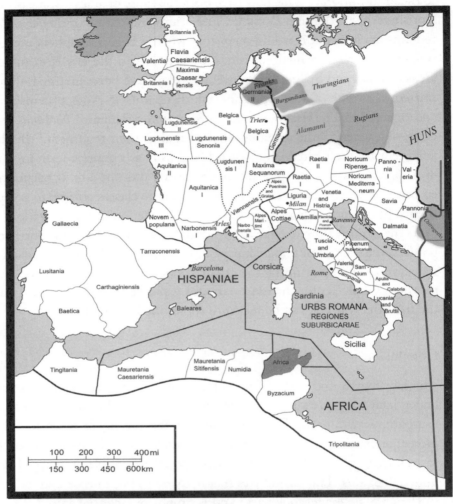

Map 2: The West c. 408: the boundaries for the tribes are very approximate.

Chapter Two

Stilicho[1]

After Theodosius I had won the Battle of the Frigidus in 394 the Empire had been reunited under the rule of one emperor. The unification was to be short-lived: Theodosius died due to a disease including severe oedema (dropsy) on 17 January 395. Once again the Empire was divided, this time between Theodosius' sons: Arcadius in the East and Honorius in the West. Honorius' brother-in-law Stilicho took control of the Western army, as at this point Honorius was still only 10 years of age. It is probable that after Theodosius died Constantius became one of the major figures in the Western Army but, as the sources are focused upon Stilicho, Constantius is not mentioned.

Once in power, Stilicho began making mistakes. One was his disbanding of the *foederati* ('foreign' troops serving as part of a *foedus*, 'treaty'), in this case especially Goths serving under their own leaders following the Treaty of 382. These troops had been the first wave of attack at the Battle of the Frigidus and accordingly had suffered heavy casualties. Consequently, there was a feeling among the *foederati* that they had been used.[2] Feeling that their services deserved more reward, almost immediately many, if not all the *foederati* rebelled and ravaged the country through which they passed.

A further mistake by Stilicho was that he claimed Theodosius had appointed him *parens principum* (guardian) of both Honorius in the West and Arcadius in the East. Obviously this was rejected by the ministers in control of Arcadius' court.[3] The result was an increase in tension between East and West, with Arcadius' ministers now suspicious of Stilicho's motives for any actions, especially with regard to his interfering in 'Eastern' affairs.

Alaric and Illyricum

Although balked in the East, Stilicho now took control of Italy, Hispania, Gaul and Africa: Illyricum (and Britain) were not included in his domains, at least according to Zosimus.[4] Until the Battle of Adrianople in 378 Illyricum had been part of the Western Empire. Only after that defeat was Illyricum allotted to the East by Gratian in order that the new emperor Theodosius should have an undivided command in the area and so be better able to face the Goths.

There were two major problems with this decision. One was that Illyricum was unimportant to the East so it was in effect neglected, which left the West open to attack across the Julian Alps. The second was that the angry *foederati* who Stilicho had just dismissed had been settled there after the Treaty of 382, meaning that Stilicho now had a frontier with openly hostile barbarians.

One of the leaders of the *foederati* was a man named Alaric. He had probably been given the title *Comes rei militaris* (Count of the Military) after Theodosius' victory at the Frigidus, but like most barbarian leaders his aim was to reach a higher rank in the Roman army, one that would give him command of regular troops as well as his own followers and that would bring him into line with other barbarian leaders serving in the army.[5] No such appointment was offered, so Alaric became leader of the disaffected Gothic troops.

Once he had left Italy via the Julian Alps, Alaric moved towards Constantinople and arrived at the walls unopposed: the main Eastern army tasked with defending the region had been used by Theodosius to attack the West and so was still with Stilicho in Italy. Unable to defend themselves, the authorities in Constantinople paid Alaric a subsidy to retire from the city.[6] Alaric left the region and moved into Macedonia.

Stilicho

Surprisingly, Stilicho moved with the combined armies of the East and West to confront Alaric in the Balkans. Constantius may have taken part in the campaign alongside Stilicho, or he may have been left in the West as part of a small holding force prepared to defend the West against a barbarian attack along the Rhine. Stilicho pursued Alaric and caught him at the River Peneus. Stilicho was on the point of destroying Alaric when orders arrived from Arcadius in Constantinople demanding the return of the Eastern contingent of Stilicho's army.[7] Stilicho was frustrated at the very moment of his triumph and unwillingly dispatched the Eastern forces back to Constantinople before retiring with the Western troops to Italy. Here he found it necessary to campaign along the Rhine, while Alaric – free from pressure – terrorized Greece.

397

Despite this, Stilicho hadn't forgotten Alaric. In 397 Stilicho led his Western army east again and within a short time Alaric had been trapped on Mount Pholoe in Arcadia.[8] This time the Eastern emperor Arcadius sent an order telling Stilicho to leave Greece.[9] This time, with a solely Western army, Stilicho ignored the order and continued to attack Alaric. In desperation, Arcadius now declared Stilicho *hostis publicus* (public enemy).[10] Finally succumbing to the inevitable, Stilicho returned to Italy, leaving Alaric free to continue his depredations.

Stilicho's decision may have been affected by events in Africa. In 396 Gildo, the governor of Africa, changed his allegiance from Stilicho and the West to Arcadius and the East. In 397 Gildo reduced the supplies of grain to Rome. Preparing to cross to Greece, Stilicho had been compelled to organize supplies of food to be transported from Gaul and Hispania to compensate for the shortfall before moving against Alaric.[11]

As the political and supply crisis deepened, Stilicho restored the right of *senatus consultum* to the Senate in Rome.[12] The *senatus consultum* was an ancient privilege whereby the Senate was allowed to pass laws. This right had been abrogated by the emperors, much to the dismay and annoyance of the Senate.[13] The decision, alongside other contemporary events, demonstrates Stilicho's awareness of his own weakness: he could not afford to alienate the Senate, since he would need their support to maintain his position in the years ahead. The increasing reliance upon the Senate would be a factor that would grow in importance throughout the fifth century.

Unwilling to lead a campaign in person, Stilicho appointed Mascezel, the brother of Gildo, to lead an invasion of Africa. The invasion was a complete success. Gildo was defeated and committed suicide. Mascezel quickly restored the supply of grain to Rome and one of Stilicho's problems was thus removed.

In the meantime, thanks to his continued pressure in the Balkans, Alaric had finally managed to secure the post of *magister militum per Illyricum*

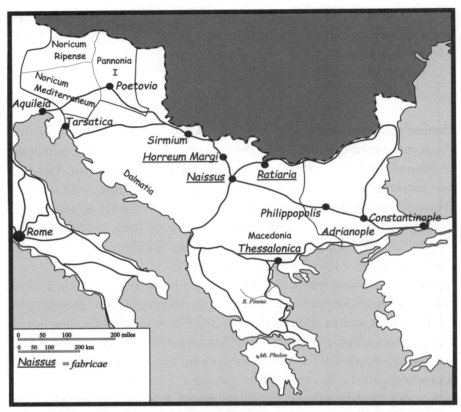

Map 3: Alaric as *magister militum per Illyricum* with associated *fabricae*.

(Master of the Troops in Illyricum) from the East. In his new post he was able to exercise jurisdiction as a regular Roman officer, which no doubt enhanced his reputation among his followers.[14] More importantly, he also took control of the imperial *fabricae* (arms factories) at Thessalonica, Naissus, Ratiaria and at Horreum Margi in Moesia Secunda.[15] Using these factories he was able to extensively equip his men with Roman-made equipment and he may have been able to secure horses in order to improve the quality of his cavalry. More importantly for Alaric, from 397 to 400 he was able to relax a little and reap the rewards of his actions.

Honorius and Maria

In the West, in order to further secure his position, in 398 Stilicho married his c.12-year-old daughter Maria to the 14-year-old emperor

Honorius.[16] With his role as father-in-law cemented, Stilicho spent the next two years ensuring that his position in the West remained strong, and defending the borders from barbarian incursions. However, these campaigns demonstrated that one shortage he continually faced was new recruits for the army.

In these years, relations between East and West remained poor. However, the rise and fall of the Goth Gainas in Constantinople had major repercussions, not least the rise of anti-Gothic feeling in the East: as events unfolded, the Goth Alaric in Illyricum knew that his position was now insecure. Paradoxically, the new Eastern regime was more friendly towards Stilicho and the West and relations improved. With the Empire once again 'united' in outlook, Alaric must have realized that in the near future the Eastern army would be turned against him. Alaric took the only course open to him: knowing that the West was continually short of troops, he offered his services to Stilicho.[17] It is possible, given the earlier enmity between the two men, that Stilicho did not want an alliance with Alaric. Events in late 401 were to prove to everyone that the West did in fact need an alliance with either Alaric or a different 'barbarian' leader who had the support of a large number of troops.

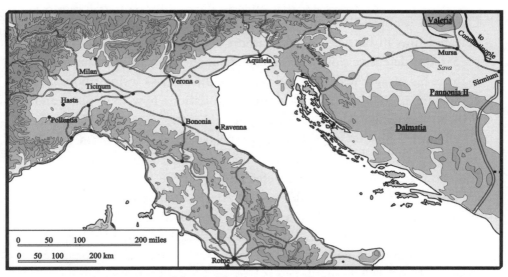

Map: 4: Alaric's invasion of Italy.

Invasions

With envoys scurrying between Constantinople, Rome and Illyricum, in early autumn 401 Raetia and Noricum was invaded by a force of Vandals and Alans.[18] Gathering his forces, possibly including troops from the Julian Alps, Stilicho quickly defeated the invaders.[19] Possibly taking advantage of the situation and there being no offer from Stilicho, in late autumn 401 Alaric crossed the Julian Alps and invaded Italy.[20] Meeting little opposition, Alaric soon placed Aquileia under siege.[21]

Stilicho, campaigning in Raetia and Noricum, was completely taken by surprise and needed time to organize a defence.[22] Realizing that Aquileia was too tough a nut to crack, in early 402 Alaric raised the siege and passed into the Plain of Venetia, advancing towards the imperial court in Milan to put pressure on the court to give him a military post. Within a short space of time Milan was placed under siege.

At the beginning of March Stilicho led his troops back into Italy and relieved the siege of Milan.[23] Preparations were quickly made for the court to move to Ravenna, a coastal city protected by marshes with only one means of access from land. The move was completed before the end of the year.[24]

With the siege broken, Alaric moved west, apparently heading for Gaul. He was too slow: Stilicho caught up with him at Pollentia and defeated him in battle.[25] Alaric withdrew towards the mountains and prepared a defensive position.[26] Despite the victory, Stilicho needed to manage his meagre resources and was unwilling to risk losing troops and equipment in another pitched battle. Negotiations now took place and Stilicho persuaded Alaric to leave Italy and settle instead in Pannonia (Illyricum).[27] Shadowing Alaric as he headed back East, when Alaric attempted to break the agreement and head north across the Alps, Stilicho was ready for him and defeated him at the Battle of Verona in summer 402.[28] Once the battle was lost Alaric attempted to break out to Raetia, but was blockaded on a hill before he could reach the mountain passes.[29] At this point, many of the troops that Alaric had led over the Alps into Italy lost faith in their leader: large numbers now began to desert to Rome.[30] Among these was Sarus, a Goth of some standing who, along with his brother Segeric, were vehement opponents of Alaric.[31] Sarus would have a large part to play later.

Alaric now negotiated again with Stilicho and was allowed to settle with what remained of his forces on the borders of Dalmatia and Pannonia, most likely in Pannonia II.[32] Sozomen suggests that Alaric was allotted *annona* as part of the settlement.[33] It is also possible that Stilicho gave hostages to Alaric at this point rather than as usually claimed in 405, although the circumstances and hence the dating are debatable.[34] As a consequence, it is possible that Alaric was made *Dux Pannoniae Secundae*, or possibly was the first *Comes rei militaris* of 'Illyricum' as claimed by Orosius.[35] Whatever the case, for the next three years he caused few problems for Stilicho.

Eudoxia and Illyricum

The thaw in relations between the courts at Ravenna and Constantinople was not destined to be permanent. Political machinations at the Eastern court ensured that affairs again took a downward turn. Seemingly the last straw was when Arcadius, the Eastern emperor, gave his wife Aelia Eudoxia the title *Augusta* (Empress) and paraded her statues throughout the East. Apart from acclaiming her as *Augusta* without the agreement of the West, Eudoxia was the daughter of a Frank, a now-deceased *magister militum per Orientem* named Bauto. Having a 'barbarian' named as *Augusta* was too much for the conservative West, who saw it as a sign that the East was in political and moral decline. As tensions grew, Stilicho refused to recognize the Eastern nominations for consul for either 404 or 405.[36]

Before the end of 404 circumstances once again intervened to cloud events. Probably brought on by the religious and political strains of the year, the *Augusta* Eudoxia had a miscarriage. It was to prove fatal for herself as well as the child: on 6 October 404 Eudoxia died. A passage from Zosimus suggests that her death resulted in political turmoil in the East.[37] With this in mind, Stilicho may have used the change of regime to make one last attempt to assert his claim to be *parens principum* of Arcadius.

In addition, it is around this time that Stilicho at last recognized the strategic, financial and military importance of Illyricum. Knowing that his claim to *parens principum* would be rejected, Stilicho decided that the East might accede to a lesser claim if it meant that Stilicho finally gave up his claim to *parens principum*. Therefore, he alleged that Theodosius was planning to return the whole of the Prefecture of Illyricum to the West before he died.[38]

The scheme did not work: the claim worsened relations with the East, but the affair may also have helped intensify opposition in the West to Stilicho's policies. Up to this date there is little evidence for any resistance to Stilicho, but it would appear to have been steadily growing. According to Rutilius Namatianus in the *de Reditu suo* (*A Voyage Home to Gaul*), opposition to Stilicho was mounting and was using the prophecies in the Sibylline Books, a collection of oracular sayings kept in the Temple of Apollo in Rome, to throw doubt on Stilicho's actions. As a result, possibly in the year 405, Stilicho had the books burned.[39] Although this story may not be true, it does suggest that Stilicho's enemies were becoming more vocal in their opposition to his rule.

Ignoring the opposition, Stilicho pressed ahead with plans for forcibly annexing Illyricum, part of which involved using Alaric's forces. There followed negotiations between Stilicho and Alaric and an agreement was reached. To secure the arrangements hostages were exchanged, with Alaric specifically demanding two named hostages: Jason, son of Jovius, and a man named Aetius. Aetius would rise to great political and military power after the death of Constantius. However, events did not go as planned:

> Stilicho, the general of Honorius, a man who had attained great power, if any one ever did, and had under his sway the flower of the Roman and of the barbarian soldiery, conceived feelings of enmity against the rulers who held office under Arcadius, and determined to set the two empires at enmity with each other. He caused Alaric, the leader of the Goths, to be appointed by Honorius to the office of general of the Roman troops, and sent him into Illyria; whither also he dispatched Jovius, the praetorian prefect, and promised to join them there with the Roman soldiers in order to add that province to the dominions of Honorius. Alaric marched at the head of his troops from the barbarous regions bordering on Dalmatia and Pannonia, and came to Epirus; and after waiting for some time there, he returned to Italy. Stilicho was prevented from fulfilling his

agreement to join Alaric, by some letters which were transmitted to him from Honorius. These events happened in the manner narrated.

Sozomen, Ecclesiastical History, 8.25, Translation:
http://www.ccel.org/ccel/schaff/npnf202.iii.xiii.xxv.html
(*March 2009*)

Radagaisus

The letters from Honorius alerted Stilicho to a new problem. In late 405 the Goth Radagaisus led a large number of people – allegedly 400,000 – over the Alps into Italy.[40] The imperial response was surprising: either Stilicho or Honorius secured additional troops from the Huns under Uldin who had settled near the eastern borders.[41] Once in Italy, Radagaisus divided his forces into three. When the campaign season of 406 began, Stilicho with his Hunnic reinforcements moved against the portion led by Radagaisus himself.[42] Taken by surprise, Radagaisus was forced to retreat to the heights around Faesulae where he was captured and executed. Some 12,000 of his men were taken into Roman service. The other two groups were quickly defeated and the remnants driven out of Italy. As usual, Constantius is not named in the sources, but it is likely that he had a hand in at least one of the military manoeuvres that took place in this year.

The overwhelming defeat and execution of Radagaisus meant that Stilicho's profile abroad was raised to a high level. There was little likelihood of the tribes on the northern frontiers taking advantage of his absence for at least one campaign season. Consequently, Stilicho returned to his plan for an attack upon Illyricum. In early 407 Stilicho ordered Alaric to march to Epirus before awaiting the arrival of Stilicho with troops from the Italian army.[43] The plan was for the combined force to annex the whole of the Prefecture of Illyricum for the West.

Again the attack would be halted. Before he could set sail Stilicho received a letter from Honorius forbidding him to go.[44] Not only was Honorius unhappy with the concept of invading the East, but there had been a new development in the West: barbarians had crossed the Rhine into Gaul.[45]

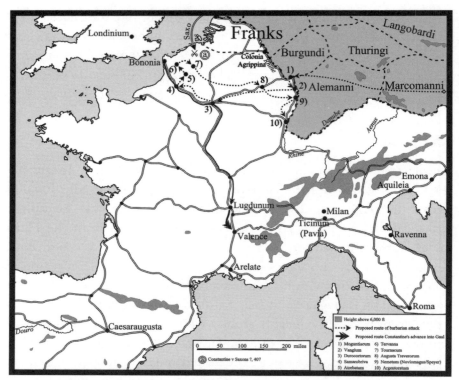

Map 5: The Barbarian Invasion and Constantine III in Gaul.

The Invasion of Gaul[46]

On the last day of 406 a large number of barbarians crossed the Rhine
frontier into Gaul. They consisted of Asding Vandals under Godigisel,
of Alans under two 'kings', Respendial and Goar, and of separate groups
of Siling Vandals and Sueves. The Alan Goar immediately offered his
services to the Romans and along with the people he led appears to
have crossed into the Empire unhindered. He is later attested as serving
Aetius.[47] Earlier, Stilicho had withdrawn troops from the Rhine to face
Alaric. Hoards found in the region occupied by the Franks suggest that
he made an agreement with the Franks to defend the frontier in return
for gold.[48] This may explain why only the Franks fought the invaders, in
order to perform both their duty as federates and to protect their homes.
The Franks were (narrowly) defeated and the main body of the barbarians
crossed the frontier: however, this gave extra time for the news of the
invasion to reach Honorius. Once he received the information, Honorius
immediately ordered the invasion of Illyricum to be cancelled.

The British Revolt

In addition, at the end of 406 the British had revolted and a man named Marcus was elected to be the new emperor. He was assassinated and his place taken by a man named Gratian. When news of the barbarian invasion of Gaul reached Britain, it was assumed that Gratian would lead his troops to the continent. He was in turn assassinated when it was realized that he was not going to act.[49] He was replaced by Flavius Claudius Constantinus, better known as Constantine III.[50]

As the Vandals, Alans and Sueves attacked the cities of northern Gaul, Constantine quickly collected an army together and crossed to Gaul.[51] He sent his newly-appointed generals, Nebiogast and Justinian, to secure Lyon, the capital of the Gallic Prefecture, ignoring the barbarian invaders. However, shortly after the capture of Lyon, Constantine opened negotiations with the barbarians.[52] By a combination of force and diplomacy Constantine brought the invaders under control and used them to swell his own ranks.[53] With Gaul secure, Constantine took measures to consolidate the Rhine defences, possibly including the payment of gold to the Frankish tribes in the north to convert them from their loyalty to Stilicho.[54] To make matters worse for Stilicho, Hispania also recognized Constantine.[55]

The Fall of Stilicho

News of Constantine's landing caused a crisis and Stilicho now had no option but to cancel the proposed campaign in Illyricum.[56] He ordered the Roman troops to move from the east coast of Italy to Pavia, yet by the time the army had been moved it was too late in the year to take any action in 407. In the meantime, Alaric returned to the Western-controlled part of Illyricum and demanded 4,000lb of gold to pay for his troops' invasion of Epirus, a payment which Stilicho forced through the Senate.

At the same time, the usurper Constantine sent envoys asking to be made a colleague of Honorius, a move that was rejected. Instead, early in 408 the Goth Sarus was given a small army by Stilicho and he quickly attacked Constantine, defeating Constantine's forces and killing Justinian and later Nebiogast, before besieging Constantine in Valence. However, new forces from northern Gaul arrived to support Constantine and Sarus fled back over the Alps. Free from attack, Constantine moved further south and conquered Arles.

At around the same time in 408, relatives of Honorius in Hispania, named Didymus and Verinianus, rebelled against Constantine III's rule. Constantine sent his son Constans, supported by Gerontius, his new *magister militum*, to retake control of Hispania. After initial resistance, Constans defeated and captured the two men and returned with his captives to Gaul. Didymus and Verinianus were later executed.

The Second Marriage of Honorius

At approximately the same time, at some point in May 408, Stilicho married Aemilia Materna Thermantia (commonly known as Thermantia), his second daughter, to the Emperor Honorius, now aged 23. Prior to this, although certainty is impossible, it would appear that Stilicho's eldest daughter, Honorius' first wife Maria, had died. The circumstances surrounding the second marriage are open to interpretation, but it is most likely a desperate attempt by Stilicho to maintain his position in the face of growing hostility at court.

Alaric and Arcadius

With Constantine III now in control of the Empire west of the Alps it was clear that a major expedition was needed to defeat him. Over the protests of many in the Senate, Stilicho appointed Alaric to the command in Gaul. As the Senate had only just been forced to give in to Alaric's demands for 4,000lb of gold, the appointment of Alaric alienated many to Stilicho's domination and opposition to his domination hardened still further.[57]

At this point news arrived that Emperor Arcadius had died in Constantinople. Honorius declared his intention of travelling to Constantinople to supervise the care of his nephew, the new emperor Theodosius II, but Stilicho quickly intervened and declared that he would go himself, probably in an attempt to install himself as the guardian of the young Theodosius. Tensions mounted, but for unknown reasons Stilicho remained stationary in Italy.

Finally, in mid-August 408, as the emperor inspected the troops in Pavia prior to the Gallic expedition, Olympius, Honorius' *magister scrinii* (Master of the Imperial Secretaries), instigated a mutiny of the army. Many leading men of Stilicho's regime were seized and killed, and the emperor himself feared for his life.

News of the mutiny was quickly carried to Stilicho, who at this time was in Bononia. Stilicho fled to Ravenna, and Olympius, who was now master of the emperor, ordered the troops in Ravenna to place Stilicho under house arrest. When news reached Stilicho of his impending arrest, he sought sanctuary in a church. At daybreak on 22 August 408 the soldiers, led by one Heraclianus, entered the church and swore an oath before the bishop that they had been ordered by the emperor not to kill but to arrest Stilicho.[58] Once Stilicho was out of the church, however, Heraclianus produced a second letter, condemning Stilicho to death for his 'crimes against the state'.[59] At this point Stilicho's servants and loyal federates made to rescue him from execution, but Stilicho stopped them with 'terrible threats and submitted his neck to the sword'.[60] Heraclianus was made *Comes Africae* as a reward for his actions.[61] Heraclianus in Africa would have a major influence on future events. In the meantime, upon Stilicho's death chaos and anarchy broke out in Italy.

Chapter Three

Italy After Stilicho

After the death of Stilicho, all court affairs were controlled by Olympius…and the emperor distributed the other offices to Olympius' nominees. A widespread search was made for Stilicho's friends and supporters. Deuterius, the *Praepositus Sacri Cubiculi*, and Petrus, the *Primicerius Notarium* were brought to trial and public torture was used to make them inform against Stilicho. When, however, they revealed nothing against either themselves or him and Olympius had wasted his efforts, he had them clubbed to death.

Zosimus, 5.36.1–2.

Olympius now assumed the post of *magister officiorum*, the most senior of all the civil positions, and took steps to secure his position at court.[1] Surviving supporters of Stilicho were questioned in an attempt to prove that he had had designs on the throne, but not all: Jovius, the Praetorian Prefect of Illyricum who had acted as an intermediary between Stilicho and Alaric, retained his post and may have led the opposition to Olympius. It is possible that the most powerful of Stilicho's colleagues – including Constantius – either joined with Jovius to guarantee their safety or had already taken steps to distance themselves from Stilicho's policies. When Olympius' interrogations failed, an edict was issued on 22 November 408 which alleged simply that Stilicho had been encouraging the barbarians (Alaric) to make trouble.[2] In the meantime, Thermantia, Stilicho's daughter and Honorius' second wife, was divorced and dismissed from court, Honorius ordering that she be returned to her mother in Rome.[3]

With the government now controlled by Olympius and his allied civil politicians, seemingly none with military experience, the threat of direct military opposition to Alaric receded. To make matters worse, indecision and infighting appears to have become endemic in the court in Ravenna as different factions attempted to oppose the sudden primacy of Olympius, whose anti-Stilicho/Alaric policy was not universally approved. The uncertainty and delay were to prove disastrous.

Constantius' location during this period is unknown. Constantius had been attached to Honorius' court and may have been seen simply as loyal to Honorius above Stilicho, despite his personal connections with the latter. This could explain why he remained safe when Stilicho was executed. On the other hand, he may have been one of those attending upon Stilicho in Bononia and so may have been able to avoid the questioning of Stilicho's supporters simply by remaining with some loyal troops who would defend him. Whatever the case, it would appear that he was in no position to oppose what happened next.

The *Foederati*

Stilicho had had very close connections with the majority of the Gothic and non-Gothic *foederati*, not solely with Alaric. Unlike the regular army officers, who at least in theory owed their loyalty to the emperor, the leaders of the *foederati* had separate loyalties and aims. Their first loyalty was to themselves and their men. Their second loyalty was to the man they had agreed to serve; in this case, Stilicho, hence their attempts to halt his execution. They had little or no loyalty to either the emperor or the empire. They now waited upon events.

What happened next would have exceeded their wildest fears. In an orgy of reprisal and bloodlust the regular Roman troops in Italy turned upon the *foederati*, probably at the urging of Olympius and his adherents: Olympius' opposition to Stilicho's employment of Alaric, and perhaps, by extension, of the use of other *foederati*, was well-known. However, as the actual federate troops were not at hand, the wrath of the Romans focused upon their families, who were located in nearby cities. All the families were either killed or enslaved.[4]

The massacre was a massive blunder. With their families killed or enslaved, the *foederati* immediately left their stations to join Alaric: Zosimus claims that there were more than 30,000 *foederati*. However, he later claims that after being joined by a further 10,000 slaves Alaric's forces still only numbered 40,000 men, so this figure is obviously far too high.[5] It is more likely that it was only some of the Goths who had deserted Alaric in 402, plus some of the '12,000 Goths' who had served

Stilicho after the defeat of Radagaisus, who merged with Alaric. It is also possible, if not likely, that the majority of the slaves who later joined Alaric were the remnants of Radagaisus' forces that had been sold into slavery after his defeat, along with many others.[6] With large numbers of new recruits, many now with a hatred of Rome, Alaric was once again in a position to invade Italy. More importantly, this time there was no military commander of Stilicho's standing to stop him.

Alaric and the Invasion of Italy

Having enlarged his army, it could have been expected that Alaric would simply attack. That he did not shows his understanding of the difficult political situation in Italy, and especially in the court at Ravenna. Instead of invading Italy, he released the hostages he had been given in 405. It may be that after Stilicho's death the Gothic hostages held in Italy had either escaped or had been released and Alaric felt he needed to reciprocate. On the other hand, it is more likely that this was a clever ploy on Alaric's behalf, aiming to prove that he was not an enemy of Rome and therefore remained deserving of a high military position in the new hierarchy being established after Stilicho's death. The hypothesis is strengthened by the fact that after releasing the hostages Alaric sent embassies to Ravenna asking for a new exchange of hostages, again including Aetius, and the payment of a small sum of money, after which he would lead his forces back to Pannonia.[7] Probably to his great surprise, his offer was refused.

The First Siege of Rome: Winter 408–409

Despite the failure of the negotiations usually being laid solely at the feet of the emperor, this would appear to be an unfair assumption. Honorius may have been emperor since 395, but he had ascended the throne at the age of 11 so in late 408, although now aged 24, he had no experience of running his Empire without the support – or probably more accurately the domination – of Stilicho. Consequently, he had not yet managed to assert his independence and remained reliant upon guidance by senior members of the court.

Due to Honorius' lack of control, the fall of Stilicho resulted in political upheavals that would endure for the ensuing two years, with ministers and generals being appointed and dismissed, seemingly at random. However, it may be possible to use these appointments to trace at least the outlines of the political machinations that were prevalent at court. At the start of this period the court was dominated by men who were opposed to Alaric being given either subsidies or a military command, not least because he had been an ally of Stilicho: doubtless they feared that, should he achieve a position of power, Alaric would attempt to punish those who had been involved in the overthrow of his erstwhile patron. This analysis is reinforced to some extent by the publication of a law on 14 November 408 restricting service in the Palace to 'Catholics', probably an attempt to purge the court of the majority of Stilicho's followers, especially those who were 'barbarians'.[8] Consequently the Goth Sarus, possibly the most able of the available military commanders, was overlooked for a military command.[9]

As part of these machinations, the court at Ravenna simply refused Alaric's request. Zosimus goes so far as to claim that Honorius 'placed all his reliance on the prayers of Olympius', although this may simply be the pagan Zosimus attempting to discredit the Christian Olympius.[10] In addition Honorius, now definitely under the influence of Olympius and his faction, appointed three new men to the highest military posts: namely, Varanes as *magister peditum*, Turpilio as *magister equitum* and Vigilantius as *Comes domesticorum equitum*. Sadly for Honorius, rather than being militarily competent, these men are described by Zosimus as being able only to 'inspire contempt in the enemy'.[11]

At around the same time Honorius sent two imperial eunuchs, Arsacius and Terentius, along with the now-divorced Thermantia, to Rome to deliver Thermantia to Serena. Yet the two men were also ordered to execute Eucherius, son of Stilicho and Serena and brother of Thermantia, a task that they quickly accomplished. Once their mission was completed, they returned to Ravenna and were rewarded with the posts of *Primicerius Sacri Cubiculi* (Grand Chamberlain) and *Praepositus Sacri Cubiculi* (Provost of the Sacred Bedchamber) respectively.[12]

For his part, Alaric appears to have been surprised and angered by Honorius' refusal to arrange a post for him. For the second time in his career, in early autumn 408 – possibly in October – Alaric invaded Italy.[13]

It has been proposed, from an analysis of Alaric's chosen route, that he intended to catch Honorius as the emperor travelled from Milan to the

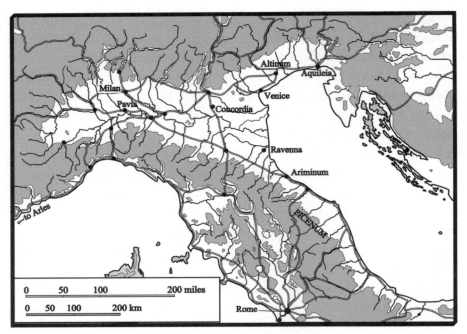

Map 6: Alaric's invasion of Italy in 408.

safety of Ravenna.[14] This is a possibility. However, another hypothesis is that, prior to his execution, Stilicho had ordered supplies to be gathered and distributed to cities in northern Italy for the use of Alaric's forces as he moved towards Gaul for the proposed campaign against Constantine III. It may be that Alaric simply travelled along this previously agreed route and that the cities along this route had not yet been informed of the change in Alaric's status from legitimate Roman commander to 'rebellious' general.[15] The second of these may be the more accurate if Zosimus' claim that Alaric advanced across northern Italy as if it were 'some festival' is in any way accurate.[16]

Following the Roman roads, Alaric 'sacked' the cities of Aquileia, Concordia, Altinum, Cremona, Ariminum and Picenum, 'destroying all forts and cities on the way'.[17] It should be noted, however, that in this context it may be more accurate to interpret the term 'sacked' as ravaging the countryside around the urban centre rather than an actual assault on the city itself. On the other hand, one or two of the cities may not have contained a garrison, with the men having been previously ordered by Stilicho to assemble prior to an invasion of Gaul. In that case, it is possible that one or two cities were indeed sacked, although if this is accurate then questions must be raised concerning Zosimus' claim as noted above that Alaric's advance was more of a 'festival' than an invasion.

This raises the further question of where the Roman troops being gathered for the proposed attack were during the period of Alaric's invasion.[18] Although it is likely that many of the troops attested as gathering at Pavia prior to their own revolt and the overthrow of Stilicho quickly returned to garrison the cities in northern Italy, it would appear from later events that some may have been withdrawn to Ravenna to protect the person of Honorius and his court. The troops recorded as later mutinying in Ravenna in 409 (see Chapter 4) may have contained at least some of the men responsible for the earlier overthrow of Stilicho, although this cannot be proved.

With the Roman troops either returning to their garrisons or travelling to Ravenna, Alaric continued on his march to Rome. En route, he allegedly met a monk who tried to dissuade him from attacking the city, a tale which reinforces the concept that at least some of the sources are focused more on the religious aspects than on attempting to analyze the actual events.[19] Finally, possibly in September 408, Alaric laid siege to Rome. In this he was aided by one major factor: the difficulties in supplying a city the size of Rome meant that Rome was constantly on the brink of shortages should there be a break in supplies.[20] Alaric simply needed to limit the food entering the city, not completely break the supply, to cause food shortages.

Serena, widow of Stilicho, mother of the executed Eucherius and the divorced Thermantia, had remained in the city. Believing that in her anger at her son's execution and her daughter's divorce she would attempt to aid the Goths, the Senate, encouraged by Galla Placidia, the sister of Honorius who had been raised by Stilicho and Serena, ordered her execution. Early in the siege Serena was strangled in the hope that, with her death and thus the loss of a possible internal agent, Alaric might withdraw from the city. The hope was unfounded, as Alaric established siege lines around the city.[21]

With Honorius and the court in Ravenna failing to act, the siege continued over the winter of 408–409, but this was not a serious attempt to capture and sack Rome: Alaric was using the siege to put political pressure on Honorius.[22] Despite the fact that the siege was a political manoeuvre, the citizens soon began to suffer, as the lack of supplies résulted in food riots and the consequent deaths from starvation resulted in an outbreak of pestilence in the city.[23]

The situation became so serious that, according to both Sozomen and Zosimus, Bishop Innocent I acceded to pagan requests that traditional rituals be performed to gain the support of the gods, but whereas Sozomen claims that the rituals were a failure, Zosimus claims that they did not take place at all. It is likely that these did take place and failed, but that the pagan Zosimus omits this information as it would damage pagan credibility.[24]

409

Eventually, the Roman citizens themselves organized terms with Alaric, agreeing to supply the Gothic forces with 'gifts': allegedly 5,000lb of gold, 30,000lb of silver, 4,000 silken tunics, 3,000 hides dyed scarlet and 3,000lb of pepper.[25] In order to achieve this total, they were forced to melt down some of the public statues made of gold and silver and remove all the metal from marble statues. More importantly, they also sent an embassy including two men named Caecilianus and Attalus, plus Basil, a provincial governor, and John, the *Primicerius Notariorum*, to Honorius supporting the treaty, asking for permission from Honorius to pay the ransom and for the emperor to agree to give hostages to Alaric.[26]

Unsurprisingly, the embassy from Rome to Ravenna was to prove a failure.[27] The opposition of Honorius and Olympius to Alaric resulted in the treaty failing to be ratified: although the court agreed to the Romans paying the money, they refused to agree to any exchange of hostages. Instead, and possibly a surprise, Caecilianus and Attalus were promoted to the posts of Praetorian Prefect and *Comes Sacrarum Largitionum* respectively.[28] Although largely pointless, the move may have been an attempt to ameliorate Honorius' refusal in the eyes of the Roman Senate, but later events suggest that Olympius may have acceded to a request from Alaric that at least some of the envoys should be rewarded for their services.

Events from this point onwards become extremely confusing and establishing the correct chronological order is impossible, not least because the ancient sources have different aims and so place their emphasis on different events without giving secure dates. What follows is an attempt to collect all the available information and form it into a timeline which allows all the events to take place, while at the same time explaining the actions and reactions of the individuals involved.

A New Regime

Desperate for any help he could get, it is possible that in 409 Honorius attempted to hire 10,000 Huns to face the Goths in Italy.[29] Although there is no evidence of the Huns arriving in 409, it is feasible that a treaty was signed between Honorius and the Hunnic leader. The net result was that Aetius was sent to the Huns as a hostage: he was to become a major player in Roman politics after the deaths of Constantius and Honorius.[30] Surprisingly, the treaty agreed with the Huns appears to have remained in force until the 420s, after Honorius' death.[31]

In Italy, the negotiations between Honorius and Alaric were still ongoing, and Alaric's brother-in-law Athaulf, who had been deployed away from the Gothic main force in Pannonia, was ordered to join Alaric.[32] Waiting for the passes over the Julian Alps to clear, early in 409 Athaulf crossed the mountains into Italy. Zosimus states that:

> When these ambassadors were arrived with the emperor, Ataulphus [Athaulf], for whom Alaric had sent, as I before mentioned, had crossed the Alps, between Pannonia and Venice. When the emperor heard of his approach, and that he had with him an inconsiderable force, he ordered all his troops both horse and foot, which were in the different towns, to march under their own officers to meet him. To Olympius, who was commander of the court guards, he gave the Huns who were in Ravenna, amounting to three hundred. These finding the enemy had arrived at Pisa, attacked them, killed eleven hundred Goths, and returned in safety to Ravenna, with the loss of only seventeen men.
>
> *Zosimus 5.45.5–6.*

In theory this was a great victory, with 1,100 Goths being killed for only 17 Romans, but there is more information here than is usually noticed. For example, an analysis of the passage reveals that either Honorius gave, or Olympius took, military command of the campaign. The latter is probably more likely as Olympius attempted to raise his prestige to rival that of the deceased Stilicho by winning a decisive victory. Furthermore, and contrary to some modern commentators, Olympius' force to face the Goths was not solely the 300 Huns stationed in Ravenna: it included the collected garrisons of many of the cities of northern Italy. Consequently, the decisive victory, with 1,100 Goths killed for only 17 casualties, is more easily accounted for, especially if Olympius used the now traditional strategy of ambush and blockade. Again contrary to modern perceptions, this episode demonstrates that Honorius and Olympius were attempting to take measures to counter the Gothic invaders rather than simply sitting in Ravenna and conceding the initiative to Alaric.

However, what happened shortly after the battle implies that there is more to this event than is apparent. For example, the question remains as to whether Olympius assumed or had been given the command. As this is unknown, responsibility for the victory is hard to assign. On the other hand, what happened immediately after may give a clue, showing that Olympius had demanded or assumed command of the army. It would appear that the main strategic aim of the force was halting Athaulf's advance into Italy and preventing his conjunction with Alaric, not simply defeating him. Despite killing many Goths, it would appear that the Romans failed in their aim; the majority of the Goths escaped the battle. Although defeated, Athaulf had succeeded in his main aim, managing to join Alaric with the remainder of his forces. Sadly, there is no indication of the number of survivors who reached Alaric's camp. Athaulf's defeat during the extended negotiations would have demonstrated clearly to Alaric that the emperor, or more likely just Olympius and his clique, was not yet willing to accede to Alaric's demands, a theory which is unsurprising if Honorius was attempting to secure reinforcements from the Huns.

Analysis of the situation is complicated by the fact that Zosimus, as quoted above, only relates one embassy between Alaric's Rome and Ravenna, but it is known that a second embassy was sent, this time involving Bishop (Pope) Innocent I of Rome.[33] It may have been hoped that Innocent would be able to exert some moral and religious authority over the emperor.[34] Consequently, to allow a sensible reconstruction of events, it is here assumed that there were indeed two embassies between

Rome and Ravenna, and that chronologically the first embassy had been sent and had returned to Rome prior to Athaulf's crossing of the Julian Alps into Italy.

In this reconstruction, Alaric and the Roman Senate had responded to the rebuttal of the first embassy by making arrangements for Bishop Innocent, the leading cleric in the West, to travel to Ravenna at the same time as Olympius 'defeated' Athaulf. Doubtless when Athaulf reached Alaric the latter would have been angered by an attack on his brother-in-law during the negotiations, but any anger he felt would shortly after have been tempered by news arriving from Innocent in Ravenna.

Hispania

While the confusion in Italy continued to unfold, events in Hispania made the situation in the West even more complicated. In late spring 409 Constantine sent his son Constans to Hispania with a man named Justus to replace Gerontius, who had remained in Hispania, as *magister militum*. Unsurprisingly, Gerontius rebelled and proclaimed his *domesticus* Maximus as emperor at Tarraco (Olympiodorus claims Maximus was Gerontius' son).[35] It is possible that Constantine had named Constans as co-*Augustus* (the dating and cause of the appointment is insecure) and sent him to Hispania with troops to suppress Gerontius' rebellion. It is also possible that a battle was fought between Constans and Gerontius, but as Constans would not have been in command of a large army at this time it is more likely that he simply fled back to Gaul upon hearing of Gerontius' rebellion.[36]

There were now three emperors in the West: Honorius, Constantine III and Maximus. In addition, at the same time the Sueves, Vandals and Alans in Gaul rebelled against Constantine.[37] According to Jerome, they quickly devastated large parts of Gaul including Aquitaine, Narbonensis and Novempopulum, but Jerome notes that when he wrote Toulouse had not yet fallen.[38]

The barbarian revolt was not the only problem being faced by Constantine. At some point in 409 Britain also revolted against Constantine's rule, most likely thanks to Constantine being entirely focused upon events on the Continent and not defending Britain from raids from either the mainland or from the Picts. Constantine had rapidly gone from being the most powerful individual in the West to one with opponents on every side.

The Fall of Olympius

Constantine's problems would not have been of great comfort to Honorius. This is because there had been a major political change at the court of Honorius. Taking advantage of Olympius' absence, it would appear that a rival clique, including several eunuchs and the general Jovius, was able to convince Honorius that the decisions and the few concessions which Olympius had made during the negotiations – possibly including the 'promotions' noted above – were not in the Empire's best interests. Furthermore, Olympius' failure to defeat Athaulf decisively and prevent his troops joining forces with Alaric demonstrated a lack of military ability. Olympius was removed from his position. Rather than face potentially life-threatening consequences, he fled into exile in Dalmatia.[39] Yet another political regime took control in Ravenna.

Chapter Four

The Year of Five Emperors[1]

Olympius had been in control for less than a year. His replacement as the leader of the court was Jovius, the same man who had been appointed as *Praetorian Prefect* of Illyricum by Stilicho in 407. Jovius was quickly promoted to *Praetorian Prefect* of Italy and then given the title *Patricius*, thus taking the place formerly occupied by Stilicho. In addition, Jovius had retained close ties with Alaric, and so Honorius – counselled by Jovius – sent letters requesting that Alaric withdraw from Rome to Ariminum, where he was to meet the newly-appointed Jovius for a new round of negotiations.[2] From his previous acquaintance with Jovius, and with the anti-Gothic Olympius removed, Alaric may have believed that fresh negotiations with Jovius would be successful.

As he marched with his forces to Ariminum, Alaric was joined by thousands of domestic slaves from Rome who preferred the uncertainty of Alaric's army to slavery and the threat of another siege.[3] Despite the resumption of talks, and possibly reacting to the earlier attack upon Athaulf's forces while negotiations were assumed to be ongoing, part of the Gothic army now blocked some of the roads into Rome and began to levy a toll on goods being transported to the starving city. They may have been encouraged in this by Athaulf in response to his recent defeat, although this is unrecorded. As soon as he heard of this infringement, Alaric issued orders to stop these levies and the flow of supplies into the city once again became uninterrupted.

In one respect Alaric's decision to negotiate with Jovius appeared to have paid off: after a short period of time an agreement was reached between Alaric and Jovius whereby the Goths would receive an annual supply of gold and corn and be allowed to settle in Venetia, Noricum and Dalmatia. This was a major concession, as these provinces guarded the entrance to Italy from the east. Jovius sent the treaty to Honorius for ratification, but he also included a letter with the recommendation that Alaric be given the post of *magister utriusque militiae* in the belief that this flattery would encourage Alaric to renounce at least some of these otherwise politically damaging territorial conditions.[4]

When the proposal was put to Honorius the emperor flatly refused to ratify it, declaring that he would never have a Goth as *magister militum*.[5] In this he may have been influenced by earlier events in the East: in 400 a Goth named Gainas had seized power, using the post of *magister militum* to gain control of Constantinople. It had taken force to evict Gainas from the city and it may be that Honorius was worried that Alaric would similarly attempt to take complete control of the West.

Surprisingly, following Honorius' rejection Jovius and his entourage now took an oath never to make peace with Alaric.[6] This decision is a little odd, since until this point Jovius appears to have been following Stilicho's old policy of appeasement. It is probable that Jovius felt the move was necessary in order to maintain his position at court in the face of continued opposition to the employment of Alaric, both by Honorius and the Senate in Ravenna.

Alaric immediately made a more moderate offer.[7] The fact that the court in Ravenna had taken an oath never to accept Alaric was a determining factor in the ensuing decision to reject the new proposal. However, at least in part the decision may also have been due to the fact that as far as Honorius' court was concerned Alaric's second, more moderate offer was simply interpreted as a sign of Alaric's weak position.[8]

Reinforcements

It was noted earlier that modern evaluations of Honorius and his court decry them for being inactive and in taking no steps to oppose Alaric, instead remaining in the safety of Ravenna. To some degree this opinion must remain intact, but in others it is not quite fair, as demonstrated both by Olympius' attack on Athaulf and by another of Honorius' (or Jovius') recorded actions. Knowing that any refusal to ratify an agreement would cause Alaric to take further action, almost certainly involving another siege of Rome, during the negotiations Honorius (or Jovius) had sent orders to Dalmatia for five regiments of troops to redeploy to Rome and act as a garrison for the city, under the command of a man named Valens.[9] Zosimus claims that this force comprised 6,000 men, the 'flower of the whole Roman army'; however, it is probably safer to assume that each of the units had a nominal strength of 1,200 men and that Zosimus did a simple sum to reach his figure.[10] In reality, the number of troops could have been much lower.

Sadly, as the reinforcements marched towards Rome from Dalmatia negotiations collapsed. Valens now made a decision that was to result in disaster. Zosimus states:

> Their [the troops from Dalmatia] general was Valens, a person ready for the greatest and most hazardous enterprises. He disdained, therefore, to appear so cowardly as to march by a way that was not guarded by the enemy. Thus Alaric, delaying until he came up to him, and attacking him with all his forces, cut off all his troops, except a hundred, who with much difficulty escaped, together with their commander. He arrived in safety at Rome together with Attalus, whom the senate had sent to the emperor.
>
> *Zosimus, 5.45.1–2.*

Of great note is the fact that a man named Maximilianus was captured at this time and later ransomed by his father for 30,000 pieces of gold. Despite the apparent decline of the Empire and the earlier alleged melting down of statues in Rome, rich senators and their compatriots could still afford to pay vast sums of money when needed.

The Attalus named by Zosimus in the above passage was the man who had recently been promoted to the post of *Comes Sacrarum Largitionum* on the order of Olympius, now returning from Ravenna. He would play a large part in upcoming events, not least because he immediately dismissed a man named Heliocrates from his post. Heliocrates had been appointed to investigate the estates of Stilicho's supporters in Rome, but instead he had warned these people to hide what they could. The episode highlights the political divisions in Italy, with Attalus still pursuing Stilicho's supporters but Heliocrates attempting to protect them.

According to Zosimus, withdrawing troops from Dalmatia to garrison Rome was not the only attempt made by Honorius (or possibly Jovius) to secure extra troops with which to face Alaric. Even as Alaric made further attempts to secure a treaty:

Affairs having thus been concerted, the emperor called ten thousand Huns to his assistance in the war against Alaric. In order that he might have provisions ready for them on their arrival, he ordered the Dalmatians to bring corn, sheep, and oxen. He sent out scouts to gain information of the way by which Alaric intended to march to Rome. But Alaric, in the meantime, repented of his intention of proceeding against Rome, and sent the bishops of each city, not only as ambassadors, but also to advise the emperor not to suffer so noble a city, which for more than a thousand years had ruled over a great part of the world, to be seized and destroyed by the Barbarians, nor such magnificent edifices to be demolished by hostile flames, but to prefer entering into a peace on some reasonable conditions. He instructed them to state to the emperor, that the Barbarians wanted no preferments, nor did he now desire the provinces which he had previously chosen as his residence, but only the two Norica, which are situated on the extremity of the river Danube, are harassed by continual incursions, and yield to the treasury a very small revenue. Besides this he only demanded annually as much corn as the emperor should think proper to grant, and would remit the gold. And that a friendship and alliance should subsist between himself and the Romans, against every one that should rise to oppose the empire.

Zosimus, 5.50.

From this extract it would appear that Alaric remained determined to secure a post in Honorius' regime. However, a third peace proposal in a very short period of time must have reinforced the perception in Ravenna that Alaric was in a very weak position and was grasping at straws.

Sadly, both for Honorius and modern historians, there is no mention of any Hun reinforcements arriving in Italy to support Honorius, although, as will be seen below, it is possible that at least some Hun troops did arrive at Ravenna much later.[11]

Despite Alaric's more generous peace proposals, politics in Ravenna would ensure that these propositions were also rejected. Not only had Jovius now taken an oath not to deal with Alaric, but the removal of troops from Dalmatia and their subsequent defeat meant that Illyricum had been seriously weakened and needed a strong military commander to ensure that the region was safe from attack. Obviously, allowing Alaric to return to the region as an official Roman officer could result in him first securing his position in the region and then using his new-found strength to demand further concessions. An alternative was needed.

Earlier, Honorius had attempted to appoint a man named Generidus, a 'barbarian' and a pagan, to the post of *Comes Italiae* (Count of Italy) either in late 408 or, more likely, in early 409 following the changes brought about by the fall of Olympius. Generidus had refused to accept the post due to the law passed in November 408 prohibiting those not 'Catholic' from serving 'within the palace', this despite being offered immunity and the personal pleas of the emperor.[12] Only when this law was repealed would Generidus accept a post, but not *Comes Italiae*: he was given the post of *Comes Illyrici* (Count of Illyricum) commanding Upper Pannonia, Noricum and Raetia, with Dalmatia being added to his command after the fall of Olympius.[13] The episode again highlights the deep divisions and infighting at the court of Ravenna. Generidus' appointment was justified, as Zosimus praises his abilities and from this point onwards Illyricum remained quiet and free from incursions.[14] Although the situation in Italy was still critical, at least the frontier across the Julian Alps was now safe from attack.

Mutiny

Despite this positive turn of events, affairs in Italy took a further downward turn, at least as far as Honorius was concerned. Following the fall of Olympius and the defeat of Valens, the troops at Ravenna took matters into their own hands:

> The soldiers, at Ravenna, having mutinied, took possession of the port, and with rude clamours demanded the emperor to come before them. But he through dread of the tumult, having secreted himself, Jovius issued among them, who was prefect of the court, and honoured with the rank of patrician. Pretending to be ignorant of the occasion for which they mutinied, although he himself was said to be the author of it, together with Illebichus [Allobichus], who commanded the domestic cavalry, he asked them their reason for being so violent. On hearing the soldiers' reply, that they must deliver into their hands Turpilio and Vigilantius, the two generals, with Terentius,

the imperial chamberlain, and Arsacius, next to him in dignity, the emperor fearing an insurrection of the soldiers condemned the two generals to perpetual exile. They being therefore placed on board a ship, were murdered by those who were appointed to carry them to the place of banishment. Jovius indeed had commanded them to do this; fearing lest if they should ever return, and discover the intrigue that was formed against them, they might excite the emperor to punish him for it. Terentius was sent into the east, and Arsacius was ordered to reside in Milan. The emperor having made Eusebius chamberlain in lieu of Terentius, given the command which Turpilio had held to Valens, and appointed Illebichus prefect instead of Vigilantius, appeared in some measure to mitigate the rage of the soldiers.

Zosimus, 5.47.1f.

This complicated series of events yet again demonstrates that the court of Honorius was still in turmoil after Stilicho's fall, and that, despite the presence in Italy of Alaric, internal politics were still dominating events: the presence of Alaric was a problem, but was not a personal threat to either the emperor or, more importantly in this context, his court. The greatest threat to Honorius' courtiers was their colleagues.

It is alleged that it was Jovius and Allobichus who planned the dismissal of Turpilio and Vigilantius, and given the ensuing appointments this would appear to be very likely. It would appear that a second military commander named Valens, not the man who had recently been defeated by Alaric, replaced Turpilio as *magister equitum*, and Allobichus replaced Vigilantius as *Comes Domesticorum Equitum*. Jovius, who may have been the instigator of the mutiny and who almost certainly proposed the replacements to Honorius, remained as *Praetorian Prefect* of Italy and *Patricius*. He now had his own appointments in place and was in a position to dominate the court for the foreseeable future.

Second Siege of Rome

While the political and military regimes were changing in Ravenna, Alaric, rebuffed even by his old acquaintance Jovius, returned and 'laid siege' to Rome for a second time, possibly in December 409.[15] It may be at this time that, realizing that negotiations between Alaric and Honorius would fail, some Romans fled from Rome and took refuge on the island of Igilium (Isola del Giglio).[16]

Arriving outside the city, Alaric appears to have taken this siege more seriously:

> Alaric, finding that he could not procure a peace on the conditions which he proposed, nor had received any hostages, once more attacked Rome, and threatened to storm it if the citizens refused to join with him against the emperor Honorius. They deferred their answer to this proposal so long, that he besieged the city, and marching to the port, after a resistance of some days, made himself master of it. Finding that all the stores of the city were there, he threatened to distribute them among his men, unless the Romans should accede to his terms. The whole senate having therefore assembled, and having deliberated on what course to follow, complied with all that Alaric required of them. For it would have been impossible to avoid death, since no provisions could be brought from the port to the relief of the city. Accordingly, they received the embassy of Alaric, [and] invited him to their city.
>
> *Zosimus 6.6.*[17]

Some of the alternate sources are confusing, with elements of the first, second and third sieges of Rome becoming conflated in some. Yet from the evidence available, especially from Zosimus, it is possible to deduce that, shortly after capturing Portus, Alaric's demands were accepted by the Senate and he was allowed to enter the city, though his army appears to have remained outside.[18]

The city of Rome was now under the control of a Goth, but although this should have been an occasion of note, the fact that in the past 'barbarian' commanders had dominated the court in Rome means that in reality the occupation was of little importance compared to what was happening in Ravenna.

Constantine III

Honorius wasn't the only *Augustus* having problems. In Gaul, Constantine III was now facing the loss of most of his 'Empire' to rebellions and knew that Gaudentius in Hispania certainly had plans to invade Gaul and overthrow him. He would also have been aware that Honorius in Italy was in much the same position, surrounded on all sides by rebellious or potentially rebellious subjects. In order to eliminate one potential military threat, in late summer 409 Constantine wrote to Honorius asking forgiveness for having seized power and promising help against Alaric in Italy. It would appear that Honorius simply rebuffed Constantine's peace overtures. As will be seen, however, not all at Honorius' court were so dismissive of Constantine's offer.

Part of Constantine's problem was the continuous ravaging of his domains in Gaul by the barbarian tribes that had crossed the Rhine in 406. The damage they were causing was soon to end. Unfortunately, the precise details of what happened are lost. It is usually accepted that, after their 'rebellion', in early autumn 409 the Vandals, Alans and Sueves, either finding the passes of the Pyrenees unguarded or by bribing the guards, crossed the Pyrenees and entered Hispania.[19] In this model, Gerontius in Hispania eventually managed to subdue them, and although he enforced treaties where they would provide him with military support, in effect a large part of Hispania was now lost to Rome as the barbarians settled in the region.

This account may not be entirely accurate. Zosimus suggests that in fact Gerontius had succeeded in inciting the Sueves, Vandals and Alans in Gaul to rebel against Constantine.[20] Consequently, it is possible that it was as part of their agreement with Gerontius that the barbarian 'coalition' had devastated Gaul in an attempt to weaken Constantine's political position before being allowed by Gerontius to cross into Hispania to serve Gerontius' regime.[21]

It is also possible that as part of the agreement Gerontius allocated land to his new 'allies'. However, as the tribes were unable to reach an amicable agreement as to which tribe received which area, they resorted to deciding the allocation by lot. In this way, the Asding Vandals received some of the southern parts of the province of Gallaecia with the Sueves gaining territory in the northern parts. The Siling Vandals were granted lands in Baetica, while the Alans received territory in Lusitania. Gerontius himself retained complete control of Tarraconensis and Carthaginiensis. It may be that it was the need to settle affairs in Hispania that caused Gerontius to spend most of the remainder of 409 and 410 in Hispania,

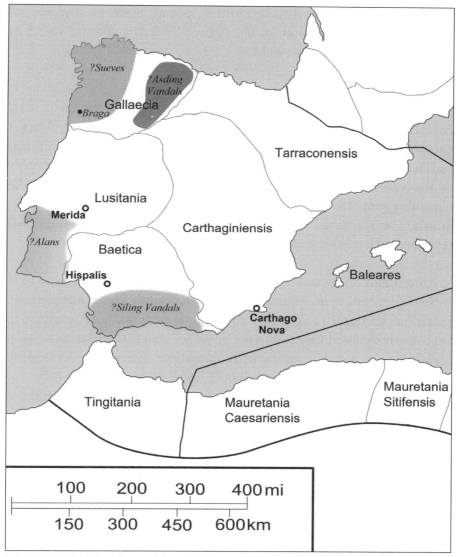

Map 7: The Vandals, Alans and Sueves in Hispania. It should be noted that the actual extent of territory controlled is unknown and open to different interpretations. This allocation is based upon events analysed later.

not least because he was arranging the settlement of the barbarians and organizing the *foedus* (treaty) that allowed him to raise fresh troops from among the barbarians to serve in his own army. It was only to be in 411 that he finally made a move against Constantine III. The presence in Hispania of three barbarian tribes was to remain a cause for concern for

Constantius when he eventually came to power; however, that was all in the future. In the present, in December 409 Alaric and the Senate in Rome drastically raised the stakes.

Attalus

After the end of the first siege, when the Senate had agreed to pay Alaric a 'subsidy', a man named Attalus had been part of the embassy to Ravenna and had been promoted to the post of *Comes Sacrarum Largitionum*, presumably on the orders of Olympius. After his return to Rome he had pursued the remaining supporters of Stilicho, suggesting that he was part of the anti-Stilicho, 'anti-federate' faction in Rome. Consequently, what happened next was extremely surprising. In the continuation from Zosimus:

> Accordingly they received the embassy of Alaric, invited him to their city, and, as he commanded, placed Attalus, the prefect of the city, on an imperial throne, with a purple robe and a crown; who presently declared Lampadius prefect of the court, and Marcianus of the city, and gave the command to Alaric and Valens, who formerly commanded the Dalmatian legions, distributing the other offices in proper order. He then proceeded towards the palace, attended by an imperial guard; although many ill omens occurred in his way. The following day, entering the senate, he made a speech full of arrogance, in which he told them with great ostentation that he would subdue the whole world to the Romans, and even perform greater things than that.
>
> *Zosimus 6.6f.*[22]

Attalus, who by now was the *Praetorian Prefect* of the city, was the new 'Roman' emperor.[23] A pagan senator, Attalus quickly had himself baptized as a Christian in order to be acceptable to the vast majority of the population. His conversion may also have been required by Alaric, who although not a Catholic like many in Rome, was still a Christian, albeit an Arian. It is probable that it was at this time that Galla Placidia was taken captive by the Goths: politically, she was a valuable asset as a hostage, and it was only now that she is mentioned by Zosimus as being a hostage of Alaric, not before.[24] She was to remain with the Goths for several years.

Africa

When news of the usurpation reached Africa, Heraclianus, the governor of the province, decided to remain loyal to Honorius, sending money to Ravenna.[25] Realizing that Rome was reliant on the grain supplies from Africa being maintained, Alaric proposed an invasion of the province by Gothic troops:

> The Romans were therefore filled with joy, having not only acquired other magistrates, well acquainted with the management of affairs, but likewise Tertullus, with whose promotion to the consulship they were exceedingly gratified. None were displeased with these occurrences, which were thought conducive to public advantage, except only the family of the Anicii; because they alone having got into their hands almost all the money in the city, were grieved at the prosperous state of affairs. Alaric prudently advised Attalus to send a competent force into Africa and to Carthage, in order to depose Heraclianus from his dignity, lest he, who was attached to Honorius, should obstruct their designs. But Attalus would not listen to his admonitions, being filled with expectations given him by the soothsayers, that he should subdue Carthage and all Africa without fighting, and would not send out Drumas, who, with the barbarians under his command, might easily have turned Heraclianus out of his office. Disregarding the counsels of Alaric, he gave the command of all the troops in Africa to Constantine, yet sent along with him no good soldiers.
>
> *Zosimus, 6.12.*

Attalus' appointments effectively created a new Roman government, separate from that of Honorius in Ravenna. Attalus had quickly become a viable Roman emperor.[26] Nor should the elevation of Attalus be seen in isolation: he was simply following in the footsteps of two major predecessors, Magnus Maximus (383–88) and Eugenius (392–94). Supported by the Senate in Rome, he, like they, was a serious threat to Honorius' regime.

Aside from demonstrating that the common perception of emperors in the fifth century as being puppets following the orders of their leading generals may not be accurate, the decision also shows that the Senate in Rome was deeply divided. The majority of the Senate sided with Alaric, wanting to send a joint Roman-Gothic force under the 'barbarian' commander Drumas. It is interesting to note that only a small part of the Senate sided with Attalus in blocking the invasion, yet this minority prevailed and only a small Roman force was sent, and it failed.[27]

It would appear that Attalus recognized that Gothic control of the grain supplies of Africa would be catastrophic, as was to prove later when the region was captured by the Vandals under their king Gaiseric.[28] Attalus refused permission for Alaric to send Goths to Africa and instead organized a campaign using only Roman forces under the command of a man named Constantine. These troops landed in Africa, but Attalus had not given Constantine enough troops: in a subsequent battle Constantine was defeated and killed.[29] The campaign was a complete failure and the province remained loyal to Honorius. In addition, Heraclianus now dispatched funds to Honorius, which the latter used to ensure the loyalty of his troops, and only now did Heraclianus completely cut the supplies of grain to Rome.[30]

Despite the victory in Africa, the pressure on Honorius continued to mount: he did not have the troops available to fight all his many enemies. In order to survive he needed to reduce the number of fronts on which he had to fight.

Jovius

Consequently, in late 409 Honorius decided that, even if his ultimate desire was to remain sole emperor, it was necessary to accept an imperial colleague in order to regain at least some control of events. Having already dismissed Constantine's attempt at reconciliation earlier in 409, when Attalus again led his army – largely composed of Alaric's Goths – towards Ravenna, Honorius sent Jovius, the Valens who was subordinate to Jovius, and others in an embassy to meet Attalus. However, if Olympiodorus is to be believed, this was no mere peace offer: Jovius had been sent to offer Attalus 'a share in the sovereignty'.[31]

If the decision by Honorius to offer a share of the Empire to Attalus is seen as being strange by modern authorities, to contemporaries it must have been astounding. Prior to 408 policy had been determined by Stilicho, meaning that there was a thread of continuity. It would appear that, after the fall of Stilicho, Honorius had begun to exert himself and determine policy. However, as he had no experience and was reliant upon advice and susceptible to pressure from his highest officials, the result was erratic interventions and complete changes of direction over a very short period of time. Doubtless this was frustrating to his ministers and was to have a large impact on events.[32]

The reasons for Honorius' latest reversal are unrecorded, so it is necessary to resort to conjecture. In some ways, Attalus was a greater personal threat to Honorius: Attalus in Rome was much closer to Ravenna than Constantine in Gaul and the presence in Attalus' army of Alaric and his Goths meant that there were troops in Attalus' army who were extremely hostile to Honorius' regime.

On the other hand, Attalus was only in command of a small part of Italy and his position would always be under threat of an embargo of the grain supply from Africa. Despite losing control of Britannia and Hispania, Constantine remained in command of Gaul, so he nominally had command of a larger Roman army than Attalus. Consequently, it is possible to assume that Honorius believed Attalus was the lesser threat and that he could be eliminated once the other usurpers had been dealt with. However, by accepting Attalus Honorius was also, by extension, accepting Alaric, and many in the court had vowed never to deal with Alaric again.

Whatever the reason for the decision, it was rendered pointless: Attalus refused the proposal, instead offering not to harm Honorius and to give him the choice of where to live in his retirement. Again according to Olympiodorus, at this point Jovius interceded and suggested that Honorius should at least be mutilated in one limb.[33] Although the suggestion was rejected by Attalus, who noted that emperors who willingly resigned should not be harmed, it would appear that Jovius had, understandably, become frustrated with Honorius.[34] Reaching breaking-point, Jovius defected, deserting Honorius and accepting the title of *patricius* from Attalus, simultaneously negating his vow never to deal with Alaric.[35]

Jovius' defection resulted in a change in Attalus' court:

Alaric for a time wished to abide by the oaths he had given Attalus. Valens, the *magister equitum*, was suspected of treason and killed. Alaric then attacked all those cities in Aemilia which had refused to accept Attalus as emperor. After easily bringing over the others, he laid siege to Bononia, but it held out for many days and he could not take it. So he went on to Liguria to force it to recognise Attalus as emperor.

Zosimus, 6.10.

The information that Valens, Attalus' *magister militum*, was killed is not very surprising. The defection of Jovius meant that Attalus now had three senior military commanders but only two posts: *magister peditum* and *magister equitum*. Alaric, as the 'senior' commander, was *magister peditum*, but as Jovius was a far more powerful individual than Valens and had had a long relationship with Alaric, it was obvious that Jovius would replace Valens as *magister equitum*. The only surprise is that an accusation of 'treachery', followed by execution, was necessary to make the change.

The defection of Jovius would have raised Attalus' cause to new heights and Alaric now began to pressure cities in the north of Italy in an attempt to force them to change allegiance, a process that began to bear fruit. The information that Jovius had defected and that Italian cities were changing allegiance doubtless raised further tensions in Honorius' court, where the defection resulted in yet further changes.

Eusebius and Allobichus

Jovius' place at the head of Honorius' court was now taken by the *praepositus sacri cubiculum*, a eunuch named Eusebius.[36] Any changes in policy Eusebius attempted to put in place are unknown, as the sources record very little about him. His domination was to be short-lived: at an unknown date, probably in late 409 or very early in 410, Allobichus, the *Comes domesticorum equitum*, had Eusebius clubbed to death in front of the emperor.[37]

Allobichus now took the position of *magister equitum* and assumed control of Honorius' political policies. With Attalus remaining hostile and with Jovius and Alaric now acting as Attalus' military commanders, it was clear that Honorius had to look elsewhere for support. Under the guidance of Allobichus, Honorius changed his mind – or had his mind changed – and this time offered to accept Constantine in Gaul as his imperial colleague. After a round of negotiations Honorius officially recognized Constantine, sending him an imperial robe and possibly granting him the consulate.

Honorius, Attalus, Constantine, Constans and Maximus: 410, the Year of Five Emperors

The narrative above clearly shows that events in Italy between late 409 and 410 are extremely confused. This is due in part to the sources' failure to include dates, but is mainly because of the fragmentary nature of the information they include. The net result is that when it comes to describing what happened in this short period there is a wide variety of possibilities. Consequently, what follows here is – as usual – based upon a collation of the sources and an assumption of what may be the most likely course of events.

Over the winter of 409–410 Constantine in Gaul made preparations for a campaign in Italy in support of Honorius. It may be as part of these preparations, rather than upon hearing of the revolt of Gerontius in Hispania, that he promoted his son Constans to the post of co-*Augustus*.[38] There were now five separate *Augusti*: Honorius and Attalus in Italy; Constantine and his son Constans in Gaul; and Maximus (supported by Gerontius) in Hispania.

The circumstances surrounding the decision by Constantine to make Constans *Augustus* are unknown, but from later events it is possible that the appointment was made in agreement with Honorius in Ravenna, or at least after correspondence with the *magister equitum* Allobichus. It would appear that at this point Allobichus' grip on his position was secure and that he feared no opposition to his policies; however, all that was to change.

Constantius

Early in the New Year Alaric and Attalus again moved to Ariminum, effecting a partial siege and putting ever-increasing pressure on Honorius. Talks again began and, according to Sozomen, Honorius was in such dire straits mentally that he had prepared a small fleet in Ravenna on which he could flee to Constantinople when he felt things were unsustainable.[39] With Honorius' resolve wavering, at this vital moment 4,000 troops arrived unexpectedly from Constantinople in the night: Honorius' resolve strengthened and he remained in Ravenna.[40]

The timing of the reinforcements could not have been much better and can be seen as evidence of continuous co-operation between East and West whenever circumstances allowed.[41] Although no details are given by any of the sources, the implication is that Honorius had been negotiating for some time with the East in an attempt to gain military support for his flagging regime. Yet if this hypothesis is accepted, two further possibilities emerge for explaining what happened next. One is simply that Honorius had sent an unknown envoy to the East requesting military aid for his rapidly diminishing Empire. The second is that Honorius had sent Constantius as his envoy to the East, hoping that he could use the connections formed earlier in his career to obtain imperial and especially military reinforcements of the strength needed to support Honorius' rule. The reasons behind the assumption that Constantius may have been involved in the embassy will become clear.

Gaining confidence from the unexpected arrival of fresh troops, Honorius stood firm and the talks broke down.[42] Of equal importance, the arrival of a large military force from the East changed the political position in Ravenna. Allobichus was no longer in control of the majority of the army in Ravenna and the balance of power now shifted dramatically.

Given what happened next, it is reasonable to assume that, whether Constantius had been the envoy or not, when the Eastern troops arrived they were led by individuals who were friends and willing to support him. It would appear that Constantius used the situation to his own advantage. With the military support of the Eastern commanders, he seems to have accused Allobichus of treachery.[43]

The nature of this 'treachery' is unclear. It is usually assumed that it was solely Allobichus' support of an alliance with Constantine, but Honorius had already attempted and failed to secure an alliance with Attalus, so as Constantine was second choice this would appear dubious. If, however, Allobichus had pressured Honorius into accepting Constantine's son Constans as a further *Augustus*, then the accusation of treachery has more weight. Although the reasons behind the conviction are unclear, the outcome was not. Allobichus was executed.

Apart from simple ambition, the reasons behind Constantius' decision to overthrow the regime in Ravenna are not stated by the sources. However, following his later actions it is possible to deduce that Constantius was confident that with control of the army, including the Eastern reinforcements, the policy of appeasement pursued by Stilicho, Jovius and Allobichus was no longer relevant. Confident of his own military abilities, he certainly believed that he could turn events around. Events would show that on the whole he was correct.

Chapter Five

The Sack of Rome[1]

Constantius

Unfortunately, there is a gap in the *Fasti* at this point, meaning that no individual is listed as occupying the post of *magister militum* in 410. Given the confusion of events during the years 408 and 409, it is possible that an unnamed individual occupied the post for just this year, but it is more likely that the death of Allobichus resulted in only one more major restructuring of the court at Ravenna.

The silence of the sources concerning appointments at court between the defection of Jovius in late 409 or early 410 and the first mention of Constantius as *magister militum* in 411 is probably due to events at court in the period.[2] Rather than conducting military manoeuvres against his enemies or conducting convoluted political negotiations with Attalus, Alaric or Constantine, Constantius may simply have used his new position both to appoint his own candidates to other positions of influence and to eliminate anyone suspected of being sympathetic to Attalus, Alaric, Jovius, Constantine or Allobichus. Only then could he consider leaving the court and leading the Roman army against Honorius' enemies. These internal events were of little interest to contemporary writers when compared to wider events in Rome/Italy, southern Gaul or Hispania.

Constantine III

Not yet aware of the execution of Honorius' *magister equitum* Allobichus, and probably in accordance with his agreement with Allobichus, in early 410 Constantine crossed the Alps into Liguria.

Due to the lack of clarity in the sources, the course of his advance is unknown. It is possible that the alliance had been agreed with Allobichus and when he learned of the latter's execution Constantine simply withdrew. It is also possible that, rather than retiring, Constantine advanced into an ambush prepared by Alaric, and it was only after being defeated that

Constantine retreated to Gaul, but as this is nowhere mentioned in the sources the hypothesis must remain conjectural.[3]

Possibly the most logical explanation is that Constantine had reached an agreement with Allobichus and so led his forces into Italy to join with troops from Ravenna and then face Alaric in battle. Sadly for both Honorius and Constantine, the overthrow of Allobichus resulted in confusion and disputes at Ravenna and the failure to send troops to join Constantine. Without their support, Constantine was unwilling to face Alaric and so withdrew.[4] It is suggested by Sozomen that Constantine's 'invasion' of Italy was an attempt at extending his own dominions over the peninsula, but this is unlikely due to his knowledge of the difficulty he would face in fighting the armies of both Alaric and Honorius, so Sozomen's account is here discounted.[5]

The 'Third Siege' and Sack of Rome

Whether a battle was fought or not, Alaric would by now have known that Honorius had come to terms with Constantine. In addition, thanks to the Eastern reinforcements it was clear that Honorius was definitely safe in Ravenna, and Alaric may even have believed, or been led to believe – the possibility of Honorius spreading false information should not be discounted – that further reinforcements were coming from the East.[6] In these circumstances Alaric was now certain that Attalus had little hope of becoming sole emperor and definitely would not be accepted as joint ruler by Honorius.

Returning to Rome, Alaric again proposed that a combined force of Romans and Goths be sent to Africa in order to secure control of the grain supply. Again Attalus and the Senate refused to comply with the request. Alaric was doubtless frustrated by the opposition to his plans.[7] On the other hand, obviously the overthrow of Allobichus was probably a sign of yet another change in policy. Moreover, the new regime was probably headed by Constantius, who earlier may have been one of Stilicho's main supporters. Therefore, it would seem that a new agreement with Ravenna was again a possibility.

At the same time, it would appear that, despite being given a senior post by Attalus, Jovius had begun to undermine Attalus, attempting to detach Alaric from supporting his appointed *Augustus*.[8] It may even be now that Valens, appointed as *magister equitum* by Attalus, was executed for 'treachery'. The sources do not give any indication of the form of this treachery, but it is possible that the charge was invented by Jovius in his attempts to secure his own position. Although he had defected to Attalus, Attalus had no senior position to offer: the posts of *magister peditum* and *magister equitum* were held by Alaric and Valens. Jovius may have wanted to eliminate Valens in order to take his place.

It would appear that Jovius was also involved in Alaric's next decision. In summer 410 Alaric deposed Attalus in the hope that the concession would encourage further negotiations with Ravenna.[9] The decision appears to have worked:

> Soon after, Alaric stationed himself among the *Alpes*, at a distance of about sixty stadia [c.8 miles] from Ravenna, and held a conference with the emperor concerning the conclusion of a peace.
>
> *Sozomen 9.9.2.*

This paragraph by Sozomen has caused a little confusion. The use of the word *Alpes* has led some translators to assume that Alaric had moved to the Alps north of Ravenna. Unfortunately, at no point are the Alps anywhere within 8 miles of Ravenna. Others have assumed that *Alpes* is an otherwise unknown place name located within c.8 miles of Ravenna. However, it is probably safer to assume that the word *Alpes* as used here simply means 'mountains': Alaric moved to the Apennines near to Ravenna, taking a position on high ground from where he was safe from attack but could pose a threat to the city.

It is also interesting to note that in these negotiations Sozomen has Alaric and Honorius meeting in person rather than using envoys. Although this may simply be a matter of terminology rather than Honorius being personally present at the talks, it does suggest that Honorius was taking these talks far more seriously than he had with the previous negotiations.

Whether this was the case or not, outside events quickly intervened. At this vital point the 'renegade' Goth Sarus launched an unexpected attack on the unsuspecting Goths led by Alaric. The attack was almost certainly on Sarus' own initiative and was an attempt to continue the vendetta that existed between Sarus and Alaric. The attack was quickly defeated, but the fact that Sarus was then received honourably by Honorius resulted in Alaric believing that the attack had been endorsed, if not ordered, by Honorius.

The Sack of Rome

Furious, Alaric returned to Rome, a sacred city as far as both Christians and pagans were concerned.[10] On 24 August 410 his troops were allowed to enter the city at the Salarian Gate and, for the first time in 800 years, the Eternal City was sacked by barbarians, the Goths running free in the city for between three and six days.[11] The event shocked the Roman world, and doubtless when the news reached him Constantius was as appalled as all other Romans by the sack of the Eternal City.[12]

There does not appear to have been any attempt at a siege and no battle was fought, resulting in some ancient sources assuming that the only manner in which Alaric could have entered Rome without opposition was by treachery. For example, in Sozomen this was by unnamed individuals. On the other hand, in Procopius it was assigned to Alaric choosing 300 of the 'youths' in his army and having them pose as gifts to Roman senators. Consequently, these 'slaves' would, at a certain date, leave their masters' premises and open the Salarian Gate.[13] Procopius also records another rumour: that a rich woman named Proba had her servants open the gate rather than seeing the population starve.[14]

As a consequence of these different accounts historians past and present have been able to choose whichever version best fitted their own interpretation. Despite these assumptions, there remains the possibility that all these accounts have missed a salient point: as Attalus' *magister militum* Alaric was an appointed officer of the Roman Senate and therefore there was no reason for the citizens not to admit him. Although they may have known of his deposition of Attalus, they would not have known that at this point Alaric had decided that the city of Rome was no longer of value.

If it is impossible to be certain concerning how Alaric entered the city, the nature of the sack is even more unclear. Estimates of the damage done during the sack range from the event being 'one of the most civilized of a city ever' to one that was 'catastrophic' as the Goths rampaged at will.[15] The great difficulty with any modern estimates is that they have to be based upon contemporary or near contemporary sources, and these sources contradict each other.

The Sources[16]

The main complication is that the ancient sources were written by individuals who were not writing 'modern' historical narratives. Some were using the event to support their own political agendas. Others were attempting to ascertain the deeper meaning of the sack, usually with reference to the changes in religious practices over the preceding century.[17]

On a slightly more detailed level, the contemporary writers include Augustine (354–430), Jerome (c.342–420), Pelagius (d. 418) and Pope Leo I (c.400–461), who wrote very soon after the sack. Orosius (d. after 418), Philostorgius (368–c.435), Socrates Scholasticus (c.380–c.450) and Sozomen (c.400–c.450) also wrote within a few decades after the sack, but weren't writing in the immediate aftermath of it and so could place it more within a historical narrative rather than respond with an emotional or religious reaction. In addition, Philostorgius, Socrates and Sozomen were in the Eastern Roman Empire and so had a further distance between themselves and the event. Finally, Zosimus (c.500), Procopius (c.500–c.565), Jordanes (c.550) and Isidore of Seville (c.560–636) were writing a century or more after Rome had been sacked.

Due to the time lapse between the event itself and many of the sources there is a change in the nature of the explanations, mainly away from an early religious interpretation to one where politics play the greater part. In addition, it is clear from a close analysis that over time many of the writers added to the accounts that had been passed down to them, augmenting the information either with their own observations or with their own prejudices. Consequently, the biases of the sources need to be borne in mind.

Political

In the political sphere, Philostorgius, Zosimus, Jordanes and Isidore focused mainly on the political context of the sack. These sources tend to use *topoi* (sing. *topos*), 'traditional themes or motifs', both in describing what they expected the sack to have been like and, more importantly, in attributing the sack to 'treachery' or incompetence. As noted above, treachery was not necessarily a factor in allowing Alaric entry to Rome. Incompetence, however, was seen by some as being the main cause, and the main culprit was the emperor, as shown by Procopius, although he was writing much later:

> At that time, they say that the Emperor Honorius in Ravenna received the message from one of the eunuchs, evidently a keeper of the poultry, that Rome had perished. And he cried out and said, 'And yet it has just eaten from my hands!' For he had a very large cockerel, Rome by name; and the eunuch, comprehending his words, said that it was the city of Rome which had perished at the hands of Alaric, and the emperor with a sigh of relief answered quickly: 'But I thought that my fowl Rome had perished.' So great, they say, was the folly with which this emperor was possessed.
>
> *Procopius, The Vandal War, 3.2.25–26.*

Philostorgius also blamed Honorius for starting the war at the end of which Rome was sacked, specifically blaming Honorius for angering the Goths by murdering Stilicho and his son Eucherius.[18] Jordanes, on the other hand, goes back even further, noting that, although the Emperor Theodosius had made peace with the Goths, Honorius and Arcadius had immediately broken the agreement, resulting in the events that occurred between 395 and 410.

As a consequence, many historians have simply accepted that it was the incompetence of Honorius and his court that were responsible for the sack: if Honorius had been a more competent emperor, affairs in Italy would have been completely different, especially if he had taken more care in protecting Rome.[19] However, it should be noted that the political explanations only took precedence later, after the first shock of the sack had worn away, and the religious explanations had been allowed to fade. In addition, as noted above, Honorius and his ministers did make some effort to protect Rome, albeit half-heartedly and dominated by incompetence and bad luck.

Religious

In the earliest reports it is the religious writers who dominate. Subsequently, their proximity to events means that more attention is usually paid to these accounts. Conversely, it must be remembered that the versions of the sack recorded by these individuals tend to reflect their authors: in modern times many of these writers would be labelled 'religious extremists', bent on interpreting events through the lens of their religion, whether Christian or pagan.

Consequently, and to drastically simplify the arguments put forward, religious writers looked at the past and present behaviour of the citizens of Rome, interpreting the sack as a sign of divine wrath. For example, pagans such as Zosimus were noting that prior to the sack the Romans had worshipped their traditional gods and the Empire had survived for hundreds of years. Hence, it was the adoption of Christianity that had caused current evils and the sack was obviously a sign that the gods had deserted Rome. On the other hand, many Christians claimed that the sack was God's punishment for the persistence by some in refusing to accept Christ. Yet whichever side of the religious divide they were on, it was clear to the majority that the Romans had called down this divine anger on themselves.[20]

The question of what form this 'divine anger' took has also been long debated. Writing soon after the attack, and from a decisively Christian viewpoint, Saint Augustine, bishop of Hippo, describes the sack of Rome as a 'terrible time of massacre', with 'destructions, fires, acts of rapine, killings, [and the] torturing of men'.[21] Philostorgius similarly states that 'the city was lying in ruins', and Socrates, among others, expands upon this theme, noting that: '[The barbarians] took Rome itself, which they pillaged, burning the greatest number of the magnificent structures and other admirable works of art it contained...[and]... Many of the principal senators [were] put to death on a variety of pretexts.'[22]

The 'apocalyptic' nature of these accounts is notable. Yet a closer examination suggests that these men, although writing during the period of shock immediately after the sack, were living at a distance from the event. Hearing of the loss of Rome second-hand, rather than waiting to hear first-hand accounts, they used traditional *topoi* in their works, with massacres and destruction at the centre of the descriptions.

Closer in distance to Rome, Saint Jerome writes that many churches were sacked, but he claims that the ferocity of the Goths was limited by a miraculous event:[23]

One of the bloodstained victors found his way into Marcella's house. (...) She is said to have received them without any look of alarm; and when they asked her for gold she pointed to her coarse dress to show them that she had no buried treasure. However, they would not believe in her self-chosen poverty, but scourged her and beat her with cudgels. She is said to have felt no pain but to have thrown herself at their feet and to have pleaded with tears for you [Principia], that you might not be taken from her, or owing to your youth have to endure what she as an old woman had no occasion to fear. Christ softened their hard hearts and even among bloodstained swords natural affection asserted its rights. The barbarians conveyed both you and her to the basilica of the apostle Paul, that you might find there either a place of safety or, if not that, at least a tomb.

Jerome, Epistle 127.13.

Marcella died shortly after the sack in 410.

In a similar vein, a few years later, Orosius wrote of an elderly woman in a church: 'a powerful person and a Christian... [and a Goth] ...asked her respectfully for gold and silver'. She gave him what he asked for:

Now the barbarian, stirred to religious awe by the fear of God and by faith of the virgin, reported these matters by messenger to Alaric, who immediately ordered that all the vessels, just as they were, be brought back to the basilica of the Apostle, and that the virgin also, and with her all Christians who might join her, be brought to the same place under escort.[24]

It would appear that soon after the sack it was being recognized that this was not a sack in the traditional manner.

There is further confirmation that the sack was limited. Shortly after his first description of the sack as being 'terrible', Augustine gives a different account:

The savagery of the barbarians took on such an aspect of gentleness..... Let us hope that no one with any sense will ascribe the credit for this to the brutal nature of the barbarians. Their fierce and savage minds were terrified, restrained and miraculously controlled by [God].

Augustine, De civitate Dei contra paganos 1.7.

Sozomen also notes that the city suffered only a limited sack, and claims that Alaric allowed St Peter's Basilica to be used as a sanctuary.[25] Agreeing with the quote from Jerome above, Orosius adds St Paul's to St Peter's, claiming Alaric wanted to save lives, and he also claims that the sack was limited, with the main damage being caused by fire.[26] Orosius even claims that Alaric commanded his troops to 'refrain from shedding blood' altogether.[27]

From this analysis, it would appear that when the news first spread people assumed that Alaric had let his Goths loose on the city, giving them leave to ravage both the city and its inhabitants. Once the initial shock had passed and a more detailed description of events had circulated, it was accepted that Alaric had restrained his troops and only limited damage had been done to the city or the people, although the Goths had looted a large amount of treasure from the city.

As partial confirmation, writing centuries after the event, Jordanes – writing a 'Gothic' history obviously biased towards the Goths – states that: 'When [the Goths] finally entered Rome, by Alaric's express command they merely sacked it and did not set the city on fire, as wild peoples usually do, nor did they permit serious damage to be done to the holy places.' On the other hand, the Christian Isidore of Seville appears to have relied more upon his earlier predecessors and writes that the sack was more violent and that 'none of the Romans who would be found in Christ's places would be treated according to the laws of war.'[28]

Despite this later reversion to the sack being seen as violent, it should be noted that the Romans themselves quickly recovered from it: writing just over thirty years later, in a sermon delivered in 442, bishop (Pope) Leo I attests that Christians held an annual commemoration of the attack, where 'the whole body of the faithful [came] together to give thanks to God for the day of [their] chastisement and [their] liberation.'[29] Very quickly it would appear that Christians accepted that God was punishing them for their lack of faith.

Taking all the above observations into account, it is possible to suggest that the sack itself involved little in the way of a traditional taking of a city. Damage was limited to accidental fires and the majority of the personal attacks were made by individuals, possibly some of the former slaves who had joined Alaric after his earlier siege taking revenge on their former masters. It is only men living at a distance and learning of the sack from survivors or travellers with lurid tales to tell who reported these tales or who used existing *topoi* from which to manufacture their accounts. Later, the severity of the sack was acknowledged as being limited and attention turned to who was responsible, with Honorius being seen as the main culprit. Even down to the modern period, these accounts have been repeated by historians intent upon reinforcing their own interpretations. Despite these differences, all are agreed with the outcome of the sack.

Consequences of the Sack

Prior to 410, and despite the adoption of Christianity by the emperor, even the Christians at the court had reverence for the 'Romans of Rome' and there existed a mutual respect between the vast majority on both sides. In reality, Christians and pagans had tended to live in relative harmony, and there are numerous examples of intermarriage between Christians and pagans. It was only after the Sack of Rome that the analyses of the causes behind the sack, and especially the religious interpretations favoured by the extremists on both sides of the debate, tended to crystallize the division between Christianity and paganism.[30]

As noted above, politically, the sack was seen by many as being the responsibility of Honorius and the court at Ravenna. Few, if any, blamed Alaric. Yet politically the sack was the final act in Alaric's attempt to secure a post in the Roman hierarchy: his actions were not those of a 'foreign enemy, but that of a Roman military officer using extreme tactics in his negotiations for another command with the government of the emperor Honorius'.[31]

Rather than being seen as a sign of strength, the sack should be interpreted as Alaric's recognition of failure. There was now no way that he could obtain a military post with Honorius, as politically Honorius could not negotiate with the man who had sacked Rome. The question now was what course Alaric would take after the sack, how this would impact the court and the rule of Honorius, and what actions Honorius and the court would take to regain control of the Empire.

Chapter Six

Constantius

After the Sack

Once Alaric had finished with Rome he left the region and headed south. Socrates, the only source that gives a reason for Alaric's decision to abandon Rome, claims that Alaric learned that reinforcements were being sent from the East.[1] Although this may have been a response to rumours that reinforcements were on their way, it is more likely simply that there was no reason for him to stay. Once he had sacked the city, Rome was useless as a political tool. He had done his 'worst' and could no longer use the city as a 'hostage'. In addition, the Senate would no longer acquiesce in his claim to have a military post within the Roman hierarchy. Despite losing the city, Alaric was not yet willing to relinquish all his hostages: he took Galla Placidia with him.[2]

In the meantime, Innocent, the bishop of Rome, established himself in Ravenna, almost certainly to remain in constant contact with Honorius to petition for help for Rome.[3] It may be Innocent's intervention that paved the way for Honorius and the Roman Senate to begin repairing relations. Honorius quickly granted an amnesty to all those in Rome who had supported Attalus, allowing them to keep their rank and office.[4] In part this was necessary, as Honorius needed to re-establish his position following the sack.

Once the position in Rome stabilized, Honorius, as noted probably prompted by Innocent, ensured that restoration work was begun to repair the damage inflicted in the sack. Apart from the social and cosmetic aspects, the work involved in the renovations helped to increase co-operation between the court in Ravenna and the Senate in Rome, helping to repair the political damage caused by Attalus' elevation. In fact, restoration work in the city continued until the end of Honorius' reign.[5]

The 'Rescript of Honorius'

It is possible that a letter issued by Honorius may acknowledge that the court recognized its own weakness, and at the same time may prove that no reinforcements were coming from the East:

> Honorius, having sent letters to the cities of Britannia, counselling them to be watchful of their own security, and having rewarded his soldiers with the money sent by Heraclianus, lived with all imaginable ease, since he had acquired the attachment of the soldiers in all places.
>
> *Zos. 6, 10.*

Although this translation of the original Greek was accepted for a long time, debate has raged since it was first noted that the translation may not be accurate. The rescript is noted by Zosimus in the section describing the events surrounding Alaric's invasion of Italy, and it has plausibly been suggested that the 'Brittia'/'Brettia' named in Zosimus' text may not, in fact, mean Britannia but rather either the city of Bruttia in southern Italy or the region of Brittii in southern Italy. It has even been noted that the spelling 'Brittia' is mirrored to some degree in the spelling of the name of the province in the *Notitia Dignitatum*, where it is named 'Brittii'.[6] In the context of events following the Sack of Rome, it is possible that Honorius became aware that Alaric was heading south and so sent letters to the cities in the south of Italy to defend themselves and not rely upon receiving military support from Ravenna, but the questions surrounding the rescript mean that such a conclusion must remain only possible rather than certain.[7]

What is certain is that it was around this time that the Britons 'threw out Roman officials and instead took to ruling themselves', an example which the natives of Armorica also appear to have followed.[8] It may be that, frustrated by the lack of protection, the citizens of Armorica indeed took to ruling themselves, but there is also the possibility that the change may have been due to the influx of a large number of people from Britannia, looking to settle in a safer place, although at this early date this must remain speculation. Whatever the case, the 'loss' of Armorica was a blow to Roman prestige and the economy: Armorica 'supported some of the richest landowners in the West, and it also supplied the Rhine army with food', important due to the loss of the agricultural output of Britannia.[9]

In part the inability to interfere in the Gothic march to southern Italy may have been caused by the promotion of Constantius and his desire to re-form the military hierarchy to ensure its support in the future: the preceding rapid turnover of *magistri* would have made Constantius determined to fill all the positions with men who would support him until he had made his status unassailable and this would take time.

Alaric

In the meantime, Alaric reassembled his forces and began the march south through Campania.[10] The evidence suggests that after the sack Alaric had finally abandoned all hope of being given a high-ranking post in Honorius' government. Instead, he now may have become fixated upon achieving a goal that would feature heavily in future 'barbarian' targets. As he marched south he began to assemble ships. The sources state that he was attempting to cross to Sicily, but the political and military benefits of reaching the island would be minimal.[11] On the other hand, Sicily was a staging point on the route to Africa, and if he managed to reach Africa, the granary of Rome and the main tax base for the West, he could cut both the grain supply to the city of Rome and take control of the largest tax revenue of Honorius (see Map 7). From this position of strength he could either force Honorius to give him an official position, or set up an independent kingdom of his own: his experience of dealing with the court at Ravenna may make the latter the more likely option.

As he was preparing to cross to Sicily, storms came up and destroyed the ships: it is possible that the lack of seamanship among the Goths caused them to fail to moor the ships safely prior to the storm.[12] Thwarted by the loss of the ships, Alaric led his troops north again. Before he could leave Bruttium, in late 410 he unexpectedly fell ill and died at the town of Consentia (Cosenza) from unknown causes.[13] His body was buried in the bed of the River Busentus.[14] His successor was his brother-in-law Athaulf.[15]

The reaction of the court in Ravenna to the death of the man who had terrorized them for the previous decade is unrecorded, but it is clear from the ensuing events that they did not hold his successor in the same esteem. In the immediate aftermath of Alaric's death, the focus in Ravenna shifted from the Goths in Italy to events in Gaul.

Gaul

One of the greatest problems of understanding events in the Empire at large and in Gaul in particular at this time is the confusion and contradiction of the sources. In the context of the revolt of Gerontius in Hispania and subsequent events in Gaul, the main dissenting voice is that of Renatus Profuturus Frigeridus. Although his work is lost, an extract is contained in the *History of the Franks* by Gregory of Tours:

> [Renatus Profuturus Frigeridus says]...The tyrant Constantine summoned from the Spains his son Constans... [who] ...hastened to his father.... And when they met, many days passed and there was no danger from Italy, and Constantine gave himself up to gluttony and urged his son to return to Spain. And while Constans was sending his troops forward, being still with his father, news came from Spain that Maximus, one of his clients, had been given imperial authority by Gerontius, and was securing a following of the barbarians. Alarmed at this, they sent Edobeccus [Edobichus] forward to the German tribes, and Constans and Decimus Rusticus, now a prefect – he had been master of the offices – hastened to the Gauls, with the intention of presently returning to Constantine with the Franks and Alamanni and all the soldiers.

The notion that Edobichus and the others travelled to the frontier to raise troops is reinforced by coin hoards found along the Rhine, which contain gold coins minted in the name of Constantine III. It would seem that Constantine had secured a large treasury with which to hire mercenaries.[16]

It is clear from this passage that, hearing of Gerontius' revolt, Constantine was expecting an assault from Hispania, but was not expecting any interference from Italy. Probably in 410, when imperial attention was focused upon Rome and Alaric, the new *Augustus* Constans sent troops 'forward', possibly in an attempt to defeat Gerontius; however, it is more likely in the hope that they could guard the passes over the Pyrenees and prevent Gerontius from invading Gaul, so giving time for Edobichus, Rusticus and Constans himself to travel around Gaul, collecting the garrisons together to form an army, hopefully to be supplemented by troops supplied by the 'German tribes'.

Gerontius

Constantine was lucky in that the revolt of Gerontius, alongside the need to settle the barbarian tribes in Hispania, had resulted in further difficulties and rebellions against the new regime. Finally, probably late in 410 or early 411, the remainder of the Spaniards 'in the cities and forts surrendered themselves'.[17] Assured of his position in Hispania and with the barbarians at last overcoming local opposition to their settlement, Gerontius launched an attack across the Pyrenees.[18] In short order he defeated the troops guarding the passes and besieged Constans in Vienne. The siege did not last long: Constans was captured and executed. At this point Gerontius showed his qualities as a military commander, pushing on and managing to lay siege to Arles before Constantine could escape from the city. However, Arles was a different proposition to Vienne: Constantine's main supporters were in the city, plus Constantine was able to tell the citizens that the commanders he had dispatched around Gaul would soon be returning with reinforcements to raise the siege. The city held out. Furthermore, learning of the death of Constans, Constantine promoted his second son, Julian, as co-*Augustus*.

Constantius

Unfortunately for both Gerontius and Constantine, Constantius had finally managed to secure himself in his position at Ravenna. Moreover, Constantius was a traditionalist: with Alaric dead, the new regime returned to the customary response to revolt and barbarian invasion. Constantius' first priority was the removal of the usurpers in Gaul.

Rather than remaining in Ravenna and watching events unfold, Constantius seized the initiative, gathered his army together, and with a man named Ulphilas as his second-in-command, crossed the Alps into Gaul and advanced on Arles. Ulphilas is usually seen as a 'barbarian' – possibly a Gothic – general in the service of Rome, as he is given the title *dux* by Prosper, and he was apparently in command of the cavalry.[19] However, the title *dux* may simply be translated as 'commander' and attest to his serving alongside the Roman army rather than being a part of the Roman hierarchy.

Consequently, it is possible to theorize that Constantius' new-found confidence and willingness to take the initiative was not simply that he had cemented his place at court. It is possible that at around this time negotiations with the Huns came to fruition and a Hunnic army arrived in Italy, contracted to serve for one campaign season, and that Ulphilas was actually a Hunnic leader, commanding the Hunnic cavalry who had finally arrived in response to Honorius' request to supply troops.[20] Doubtless this was not the 10,000 men Honorius is attested as asking for in 409, but perhaps 1,000 to 2,000 Hunnic cavalry which, with the 4,000 men sent from the East, gave him a sizeable army with which to begin restoring order.[21] This hypothesis would explain both why Ulphilas is mentioned by name in connection with the campaign, and why there is no further mention of him as he returned home after the campaign had ended.

The approach of the 'legitimate' military commander with an army caused a change of heart among Gerontius' 'Hispanic' troops: the majority deserted Gerontius and joined Constantius. Abandoned, Gerontius fled back to Hispania with a few loyal supporters. Shortly afterwards his remaining troops mutinied, no doubt unhappy with his settlement of the barbarians in Hispania. Gerontius and his loyal followers were trapped in a house, but Gerontius managed to keep the rebels at a distance using bowfire. Eventually, he ran out of arrows and the surrounding troops set fire to the house. Trapped, Gerontius killed his wife and his last loyal supporter before killing himself.[22]

Aware that the death of Gerontius meant they were under threat, it would appear that the Vandals, Alans and Sueves in Hispania sent envoys to Constantius or Honorius requesting that their settlement be acknowledged as legitimate, although it should be noted that the accuracy and dating of this claim is still a matter of debate.[23] Despite the further confusion in Gaul, the barbarians in Hispania appear to have remained peaceful.[24] On the other hand, it is possible that at this time it was not known in Ravenna that they were harbouring the usurper Maximus who, following the defeat of Gerontius, had fled to them for safety. It would also appear that once the information reached Ravenna, they refused to return him to the Empire.[25] This would cause friction later.

Britannia

When Constantine III had crossed from Britannia to Gaul the inhabitants of Britannia would have been hoping for the renewal of a strong empire under the dynamic leadership of a British-nominated emperor. They had quickly become disillusioned. After rapidly advancing to the south of Gaul, Constantine's rule had stagnated, and then Gerontius had rebelled in Hispania. As events in Gaul deteriorated into total confusion with usurper replacing usurper, Britannia came under pressure from external threats, especially from the Saxons across the North Sea.[26] Unable to obtain help from the Continent, the British finally gave up hope and decided to defend themselves. At some point between the years 408 and 411, but most likely in 410 or 411, Britannia left the Empire for the last time, although a vestige of Roman power would remain for some time.[27]

Gaul

In the meantime, Constantius took control of the Siege of Arles. The siege was to last for around four months, but it was not to be straightforward. This was because Constantine had earlier sent his Frankish *magister militum* Edobichus north to recruit troops from among the tribes across the Rhine.[28] Partway through the siege Edobichus returned with his new army.

What happened next is confusing, largely because the sources are not clear in their description of events. It would appear that, as Edobichus headed south to relieve the siege, Constantius and Ulphilas prepared an ambush. Taking the majority of the army, Constantius crossed the Rhône and deployed the infantry in a good defensive position to block Edobichus as he marched towards Arles. Ulfilas, in command of the cavalry, was deployed out of sight ready to ambush Edobichus.

Once Edobichus' forces had committed to assaulting Constantius' position, Ulphilas led the cavalry out of their concealment and fell upon the rear of Edobichus' army. Taken completely by surprise, Edobichus' army quickly collapsed in rout. Some were killed and many fled, but the majority quickly threw down their weapons and sued for mercy. Thanks to his need both to preserve his existing forces and recruit new troops, Constantius agreed. Whether the men who surrendered were absorbed into Constantius' army or released is not recorded, but it is certain that a

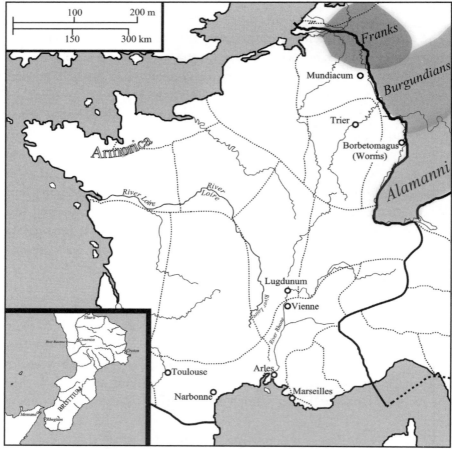

Map 8: The Campaigns and Rebellions in Gaul.

large proportion would be enlisted, not least so that they could be used as hostages to weaken Constantine's support in the north.[29] After the battle Edobichus fled and took refuge with an acquaintance, but his hope of salvation was misplaced: the acquaintance killed him.[30]

Jovinus

Possibly after the news arrived in northern Gaul of the defeat of Edobichus, but certainly after the news that Constantine was besieged in Arles and had little hope of escape, in the fourth month of the siege news arrived at Arles that the Burgundian leader Guntiarus and the Alan Goar (the latter the same who had crossed into Gaul in 406 and been accepted into Roman service) had thrown their support behind yet another usurper, an aristocrat from southern Gaul named Jovinus.[31] It has been suggested that, in accepting their support, Jovinus set a dangerous precedent, becoming the first usurper to rely mainly on barbarian rather than Roman support: the proposition was that from this point onwards barbarian leaders were to become more central in the raising and removing of emperors.[32] However, this ignores the earlier elevation of Attalus by Alaric. On the other hand, the implication that the 'propertied upper classes of Gaul were prepared to ally with barbarian leaders' would have been a concern for Constantius.[33]

The usurpation began at Mundiacum (Muntzen) in Germania Secunda, and the Franks and the Alamanni quickly added their support to the revolt.[34] Under the pretext of Jovinus' imperial authority, Gundahar and his Burgundians established themselves on the Roman bank of the Rhine with Borbetomagus (Worms) as their capital.[35]

In this context, an event in northern Gaul has received little attention: probably either late in 410 or earlier in 411, the city of Trier was betrayed to the Franks by a man named Lucius. The cause of Lucius' defection is unclear, but it seems that a man named by Fredegar as Acritus (but this may actually refer to Jovinus) seduced Lucius' wife, and in revenge Lucius allowed the Franks into Trier, effectively removing the city from Jovinus' rule.[36] On the other hand, it may be that Jovinus had used the same strategy as Constantine III, using money to convert the Franks to his cause: coin hoards found along the Rhine include coins minted in the name of Jovinus.[37] Consequently, it is possible that the entry of the Franks into Trier was with the agreement of Jovinus rather than being the treachery of a little-known figure. Interestingly, from this point until the later reign of Valentinian III, probably between 428 and 432, there are no known coin hoards found in the region: it would appear that events elsewhere in the West diverted imperial attention away from the Rhine frontier.[38]

The usurpation can be seen as marking a new phase in relations between Rome and the 'barbarians'. Taking the example set by Alaric in declaring a puppet emperor in the figure of Attalus, from this point on it was possible for barbarians, both along the frontiers or within the Empire, to appoint an emperor who would be prepared to give them land within the Empire in return for their support.

In the meantime, hearing of Edobichus' defeat and death, plus of the revolt of Jovinus (meaning that Constantine could have no hope of a further relief column from the north), Constantine realized that he had no hope of escaping the siege.[39] Instead, he first entered a church and was ordained as a priest before surrendering the city to Constantius. Constantius ordered that Constantine and his son Julian be sent to Italy, but before they arrived they were murdered, ostensibly upon the order of Honorius, who saw it as revenge for the earlier murders of his relatives in Hispania.[40] Their heads were sent on to Ravenna (arriving on 18 September 411) before being forwarded to Carthagena as proof to the inhabitants of Hispania that the usurpation was over.[41] Heros, the bishop of Arles who had ordained Constantine, was exiled and replaced by Patroclus, one of Constantius' supporters.[42]

Despite this success, it must have been maddening for Constantius that as soon as he ended one usurpation, another had begun. As Constantius settled affairs in Arles he was informed that Jovinus and a large army were heading south. However, rather than turning to deal instantly with Jovinus, Constantius returned across the Alps to Ravenna. There are several possible reasons for this decision. One is that, although in theory the new usurper needed to be dealt with first, Constantius had no idea of the size or composition of Jovinus' forces: Constantius needed time to gather intelligence. A second is that as winter was now approaching and as his men had been conducting a siege, it is likely that his troops were not in condition to fight a second battle against an enemy of unknown size, but allegedly containing men from four separate northern tribes, as well as an unknown number of Roman troops from the Rhine frontier. A major new campaign in Gaul was out of the question. A third is that, as the campaign season was coming to an end, the contract with the (hypothetical) Hunnic reinforcements was also coming to an end and so Constantius was losing a major part of his army. Finally, Constantius was being kept informed about affairs in Italy and was aware that Athaulf and the Goths were once again moving north towards the Alps. He would have been very wary of being caught between Athaulf on one side and Jovinus on the other.[43]

Despite the focus of both modern and ancient sources on Constantius, this did not mean that affairs in Gaul remained static when Constantius returned to Italy. In a rare glimpse into the intense machinations that were happening throughout this period, Gregory of Tours relays information contained in the lost works of Renatus Profuturus Frigeridus:[44]

> The fourth month of the siege of Constantine was scarcely yet under way, when news came suddenly from farther Gaul that Iovinus had assumed royal state, and was threatening the besiegers with the Burgundians, Alamanni, Franks, Alans, and all his army. So the attack on the walls was hastened, the city opened its gates, and Constantine surrendered. He was sent hastily into Italy, and was slain at the river Mincio by assassins sent to meet him by the emperor.... At the same time Decimus Rusticus, prefect of the tyrants, Agroecius, one of the chief secretaries of Jovinus, and many nobles, were captured in Auvergne by the commanders of Honorius and cruelly put to death. The city of Trèves [Trier] was plundered and burnt in a second inroad of the Franks.... At the same time Castinus, count of the bodyguard, undertook an expedition against the Franks and was sent into the Gauls.

This extract demonstrates that, although the majority of accounts only relate the affairs of the most important individuals, it should be remembered that the disputes in Gaul would have caused major divisions, both within cities and even within families. Many of the men who had supported Constantine now turned to Jovinus once Constantine had been captured and killed, in the knowledge that their lives were in peril due to their 'treachery'.

Yet despite the claims of Constantine III, and the later usurpation of Jovinus demonstrating that many in Gaul remained unwilling to support Honorius, many men in Gaul would have remained loyal to the regime in Ravenna, only waiting for a time when they could reveal their true loyalty. On the other hand, there were still others who did not want an 'emperor' to rule them, as indicated by the rise from this point onwards in the number of *bacaudic* uprisings; local leaders not sanctioned by any authority attempting to secure local rule, symptomatic of the ensuing social and political instability.[45]

Despite the ensuing problems in Gaul, and especially the setback of Jovinus' rebellion, it would appear that the military exploits of Constantius had triggered a new feeling of optimism in Ravenna and parts of Gaul, as evidenced by the list of buildings repaired in Rome after the sack of the Goths and the instant opposition to Jovinus in Gaul. In addition, the dispatch of Castinus to face the Franks along the Rhine is evidence that at least some of the cities along the northern frontier remained loyal to Honorius, otherwise Castinus' troops would have faced severe logistical problems in northern Gaul. The sense of renewal was echoed by Olympiodorus, whose history reveals a story of decline and renewal between the dates 407 and 425.[46]

Italy

While Constantius was attempting to restore direct rule in Gaul, Honorius was attempting to re-establish his authority over the rest of the Western Empire. As part of this drive, he convened a council to resolve the Donatist Controversy in Africa. Doubtless he hoped that easing tensions in Africa would ensure imperial rule in the region, as well as helping the governor to put down any uprisings.

With the retreat of the Goths from Rome, Honorius began a new policy which would become ever more important for emperors as the fifth century progressed. As the Empire shrank, the emperors were forced to seek a closer relationship with the powerful and immensely wealthy Senatorial aristocracy in Rome. This process had begun in the late fourth century, for example when Stilicho had deferred to the Senate with regard to declaring war against Gildo in Africa, and was again present when Stilicho had little option but to consult the Senate with regard to paying Alaric for his part in the ostensible invasion of Illyricum, as well as when desiring to give Alaric a permanent military position within the Roman military hierarchy.[47] The increasing reliance upon the Senate in Rome was to become a factor throughout the fifth century, although this dependency is sometimes overlooked by modern commentators, who prefer to interpret these and later events as simply being dominated by military commanders ruling puppet emperors.[48]

At the same time as Honorius was attempting to shore up his regime, the same regime was being damaged by the continuous presence of Athaulf and the Goths in Italy. Although not usually mentioned by the sources, it is clear that Athaulf was still attempting to negotiate with Honorius, using Galla Placidia as a bargaining tool, as well as continuing

Plate 1: Gold aureus of Constantius III. (*Wildwind coins*)

Plate 2: Coin of Constantius III. (*Wildwind coins*) To some degree these two coins reinforce the description given in the sources.

Plate 3: Bust of Honorius. Honorius' youth at the time of Constantius' rise is often overlooked.

Plate 4: The favourites of the emperor, by John William Waterhouse. This is the classical depiction of the emperor Honorius as a 'dissolute ruler'.

Plate 6: A nineteenth-century woodcut showing Alaric stripping Attalus of the emperor's crown. As usual, nineteenth-century depictions of 'barbarians' follow the standard image of the barbarian 'other'.

Plate 5: The traditional view of the 'barbarian' Alaric. In reality, there would have been little difference in appearance between Alaric and his opponents.

Plate 7: 'The Burial of Alaric', as drawn by H. Leutemann (nineteenth century). Many treasure-hunters have tried to locate the burial site.

Plate 8: The traditional image of the Gothic Sack of Rome (Joseph-Noël Sylvestre, 1890). The 'barbarians' are pictured naked, emphasizing their 'barbarity'.

Plate 9: 'Alaric's Triumphant Entry Into Rome': another traditional image of the Sack of Rome by the Goths. Interestingly, the ruins in the background point more towards the eighteenth century than the fifth.

Plate 10: Coin of Priscus Attalus. Although a usurper promoted by Alaric, Attalus was in a position to mint his own coins. These followed traditional designs.

Plate 11: Coin of Galla Placidia. Her marriages to Athaulf and Constantius plus her dealings with both Honorius and Theodosius II give the impression of a strong, independent woman.

Plate 12: A miniature painting on gilded glass from Santa Giulia Museum in Brescia, mounted on King Desiderius' Cross. Previously thought to depict a portrait of Galla Placidia and her children, this assumption is now disputed.

Plate 13: Statue of Athaulf at Plaza de Oriente, Madrid, Spain by Felipe de Castro, 1750–53. Despite his failure to secure his people's place within the Empire, he is still acknowledged as a man of importance.

Plate 14: Pope Innocent I (as imagined by Artaud de Montor 1772–1849). Innocent was integral to the restoration of Rome after the sack of 410.

Plate 15: Theodosius II. (*Louvre*) Theodosius' refusal to acknowledge Constantius as *Augustus* could have led to yet another civil war if Constantius had lived.

Plate 16: 'The Byzantine Emperor Honorius' (Jean-Paul Laurens, 1880). It is important to recognize that Honorius was emperor from a very young age and had to contend with men who would disregard his opinions, even when he reached maturity.

Plate 17: Honorius on the consular diptych of Probus (406).

Plate 18: Inscription of Honorius. Although Honorius reigned in the West from 395 to 423, there are few specific inscriptions from his reign.

Plate 19: Medallions of Honorius and Galla Placidia. These perhaps give a more realistic impression of two of the most important individuals in the early fifth century.

Plate 20: Roman ruins at Naissus. The birthplace of Constantius, Naissus was an important city in the fifth century.

Plate 21: The amphitheatre at Arles. The decision to relocate the headquarters of the Praetorian Prefect of Gaul from Trier to Arles demonstrates that Rome was losing control of the Rhine frontier.

Plate 22: The emperors Diocletian and Galerius sacrificing on the Arch of Galerius. (*Testus, Wikimedia Commons*) The change from the pagan Empire of Diocletian to the Christian Empire of Constantine I and his successors altered the role of the emperor at important festivals.

Plate 23: Soldiers on the Arch of Galerius. The troops as depicted demonstrate the continuous evolution of the Roman army. It is often overlooked that the Empire of the fifth century is separated in time by as great a distance as, in the UK, that between the current era and that of Elizabeth I.

Plate 24: A mural depicting Roman troops. Debate rages as to whether the troops depicted are in 'parade dress' or whether they would have worn armour on campaign.

Plate 25: The Mausoleum of Galla Placidia, Ravenna. For many centuries it was thought that two of the three tombs in the Mausoleum contained Galla Placidia and Constantius III. More recently, this has been disproved. On the other hand, the building was almost certainly constructed on the orders of Placidia.

to cause serious damage as he attempted to feed and support his numerous followers.[49]

Athaulf may not have been the only 'barbarian' attempting to negotiate with Honorius. Probably late in 411 the Vandals, Alans and Sueves appear to have reached an agreement with Honorius, although the accuracy and dating of this claim is still a matter of debate.[50] Whether agreement was reached or not, from 411 to 415 there is no mention in the sources of the tribes in Hispania causing difficulties for the regime in Ravenna.[51] On the other hand, they were still harbouring the usurper Maximus who, following the defeat of Gerontius, had fled to them for safety. They may have refused to return him to the Empire or, and perhaps more likely, neither Honorius nor Constantius were interested in Maximus and neither saw him as a threat.[52]

412

The year 412 was to be a determining one in the future of Honorius and Constantius. Over the winter of 411–412, bolstered by his victory over Constantine, Constantius further strengthened his position in Ravenna. In the meantime, Jovinus established control over the south of Gaul, minting coins in Arles, Trier and Lyon to celebrate his 'victory' and, in Italy, Athaulf finally despaired of reaching an agreement with Honorius and, prompted by Attalus, determined to cross the Alps and offer his services to Jovinus.[53] It has been suggested that Athaulf had agreed with Honorius that should he be allowed to cross to Gaul he would 'suppress the tyrants', but this is nowhere suggested by the sources.

Interestingly, at roughly the same time the Goth Sarus, who had been a staunch supporter of the regime in Ravenna, had a major disagreement with Honorius/Constantius. His *domesticus* (attendant) Belleridus had been killed, and Sarus had received neither compensation nor was anyone punished for his death.[54] Although no details are given, it is possible that the whole affair was part of the process of Constantius removing any perceived opposition, with Sarus – a known capable commander who had served Honorius before Constantius' promotion – possibly the focus of opposition to Constantius. Escaping from Ravenna, Sarus also decided to offer his services to Jovinus and so headed to Gaul to find the usurper. He may have taken a more northerly route than heading directly for the region of Arles: Constantius would doubtless have had troops watching the western passes across the Alps and so have had men watching for Sarus.

The regime in Ravenna was doubtless horrified by the thought of Athaulf joining Jovinus, but whether they knew of the plan before Athaulf crossed the Alps is unknown. Whatever the case, they would have been intensely relieved that Athaulf was leaving Italy, so it is unlikely that they attempted to defend the passes across the Alps and so stop Athaulf entering Gaul. Probably before May 412, the Goths crossed the Alps and entered Gaul.[55]

The Goths left behind them a peninsula ravaged by continuous war for three years. A few years later, in 417, Rutilius Claudius Namatianus chose to return to Gaul from the East by a sea journey, despite it being late in the season for navigation, as he was more prepared to risk storms at sea than the land journey across Italy, where 'broken and unrepaired bridges coupled with derelict inns and staging posts' made the journey dangerous and tedious.[56]

Jovinus

From the limited evidence available it would appear that Athaulf reached Jovinus' court, at this time probably in Arles, before Sarus. When Athaulf reached the court, the arrival of a new 'barbarian' group doubtless upset the delicate political balance in place around Jovinus. It is likely, though not mentioned in the sources, that Jovinus had appointed the Burgundian Guntiarus and the Alan Goar as *magister peditum* and *magister equitum*. Athaulf, accompanied by the former usurper Attalus, doubtless expected a reward for his service, but with the two major posts taken the outcome was almost certainly friction between the various factions in Arles.

Tension was not helped by the fact that Sarus was already in the area. Athaulf immediately set in place an ambush: Sarus was captured and executed.[57] The vendetta between Sarus and the family of Alaric/Athaulf appeared to be over. Yet the event caused further problems for Jovinus. Obviously he did not want potential commanders fighting and killing each other: he may even have ordered Athaulf to allow Sarus to have an audience. It would appear that the death of Sarus caused Jovinus' opinion of Athaulf to decline. He already had a poor opinion of Attalus:

Olympiodorus states that 'Jovinus was distressed by the presence of Ataulf
[sic] and in oblique terms blamed Attalus.'[58] The net result was that, as
far as Jovinus was concerned, he would prefer to listen to Guntiarus and
Goar, and that Athaulf and Attalus were seen as more of a hindrance
than a benefit.

Of more importance, but not supported by the sources, the increased
tension at Jovinus' court probably led to Jovinus following the advice of
the men who had elevated him rather than the man who had immediately
gone against Jovinus' best interests by killing an accomplished military
leader. It is likely that Guntiarus and Goar supported Jovinus in his next
political move: Jovinus declared his brother Sebastianus as co-*Augustus*.[59]

It is clear from the sources that the move alienated Athaulf, leading to
the possibility that he had both wanted to be one of the *magistri*, and also
that he suggested that Jovinus adopt Attalus as a co-emperor. Such a move
could have caused a major problem for Honorius: Jovinus could represent
Gaul, and if the Senate in Rome once more swung its support behind
Attalus, then Honorius was leading a minority of the Empire without
the financial backing of the richest men in Rome. When Jovinus ignored
Athaulf's advice, the latter was resentful and ready to be approached by
representatives of Honorius.

This approach came in the form of Dardanus, *Praetorian Prefect* of
Gaul. Given his actions, it is almost certain he had been appointed by
Honorius and was in control of part of Gaul free from interference by
either Jovinus or one of the barbarian groups along the northern border.
He now brought all his skills to bear and convinced Athaulf that an
agreement with Honorius was preferable to one with Jovinus.

Accordingly, envoys were sent to Honorius to arrange a treaty. The
alliance between Jovinus and Athaulf, then the ensuing disintegration
of relations due to the death of Sarus, plus the negotiations between
Athaulf and Dardanus and then Athaulf and Honorius took time, so it
was not until 413 that an agreement between Athaulf and Honorius was
agreed upon. Athaulf finally promised to bring the heads of Jovinus and
Sebastianus to Honorius in return for a supply of grain.[60] In addition,
it would appear that Athaulf also agreed to return Galla Placidia to
her brother, implying that the Goths at this point were suffering severe
shortages of supplies, not least due to conditions in Gaul (see below).[61]

In the meantime, with Athaulf finally out of Italy, Honorius and Constantius could take measures to repair the damage that had been done in the peninsula by the rampaging Goths. In addition, Constantius took care of one piece of unfinished business: Olympius, the man who had orchestrated the overthrow of Stilicho in 408, was executed in exile on Constantius' orders.[62]

413

By 413 events in Gaul had had serious repercussions on the region. The marching and countermarching of several armies over the previous years, plus the ravages of the Alans, Sueves and Vandals before their entry into Hispania, plus the encroachment of the tribes – especially the Franks and the Burgundians – along the Rhine had caused major dislocation. The sources record that by 413 Gaul was suffering from a severe famine.[63]

In the New Year Athaulf and Honorius finally came to an agreement. Athaulf was to turn against Jovinus and return Galla Placidia in return for grain: the suggestion that at this early date the agreement also included a clause in which they were to be given land in Aquitania is feasible but not confirmed by any of the sources.[64] Athaulf quickly defeated the army supporting the usurpers and captured Sebastianus, who was swiftly beheaded. Jovinus fled to Valentia (Valence) where Athaulf laid him under siege. The siege was short-lived: Athaulf's troops stormed the city, capturing Jovinus, who was sent to Narbonne.[65] Here, Dardanus had him executed and the heads of both Jovinus and Sebastianus were sent to Honorius in Ravenna.[66] According to Sidonius Apollinaris, the murder of Jovinus earned Dardanus an 'evil reputation amongst the Gallic aristocracy'.[67]

Although Athaulf had kept his side of the agreement, thanks to events in Africa Honorius failed to keep his. In Africa the governor Heraclianus had supported Honorius throughout the years when Alaric and Athaulf had been ravaging Italy, not least by withholding grain supplies to Rome when the Senate had elevated Attalus to *Augustus*. Nominated in 412, in 413 Heraclianus was made consul as a reward for his support against Attalus in 409 and 410. Despite this, in either late 412 or more likely in early 413, Heraclianus cut the grain supply to Italy. Why he acted in this way after serving the regime faithfully for so long is not recorded. However, there are several possible causes.

Firstly, in 408 Heraclianus had killed the *magister militum* Stilicho and his reward had been promotion to the rank of *Comes Africae*. Now that Constantius had secured control in Ravenna, doubtless Heraclianus feared for his own safety, expecting Constantius to order his arrest as revenge for the death of Stilicho: Constantius had recently ordered the execution of Olympius, the other major player in the downfall of Stilicho and the man who had appointed Heraclianus as *Comes Africae*.[68] Secondly, his authority in Africa was already being undermined: also in 412, a decree had been issued in Ravenna concerning the appointment of tribunes to track down deserters.[69] Although addressed by Honorius to Constantius, it was interpreted by Heraclianus – probably correctly – as the beginning of an attempt to limit his power and finally remove him.

On the other hand, it is possible that the emperor Honorius was attempting to balance the influence of the two most powerful individuals in the West in order to give himself some level of autonomy. In 412 he had given Constantius a certain level of authority in Africa, certainly against Heraclianus' wishes, by the decree already mentioned in which Constantius is ordered to halt the process of tribunes searching for deserters. As a counterbalance, and also in 412, Heraclianus was nominated as consul. It would appear that Honorius was bidding to free himself from the domination of any single individual. In some way supporting this theory is the fact that Heraclianus is not named as a usurper in documentation issuing from Ravenna, despite other sources stating that he was attempting to claim the throne.[70] Instead, he is named simply as *hostis publicus* (public enemy).[71] Heraclianus does not seem to have made any claim to be *Augustus*.

Whatever the truth of the matter, rather than waiting for Constantius to obtain full control and order his removal and (probably) execution like Olympius, Heraclianus decided to strike first. Possibly assuming that Constantius and the main army were in Gaul dealing with the usurpers and Athaulf, Heraclianus may have believed that a swift landing in Italy and a march on Ravenna would give him control of Honorius and allow him to remove Constantius.[72] In this manner he set a precedent that would later be followed by Felix, Aetius and especially Boniface.[73]

Accordingly, Heraclianus assembled the troops in Africa and invaded Italy.[74] Events show that he had severely miscalculated. Although he only had the few troops from Africa, he doubtless expected the remaining army in Italy to either change allegiance or at least refuse to fight him: the fact that he was now consul, demonstrating that Constantius was not yet in complete control, may have convinced him that the army would join him.[75] He was to be disappointed. Marching along the *Via Flaminia*, he was defeated at the Battle of Utriculum by the *comes* Marinus with heavy casualties and fled back to Africa.[76] Shortly afterwards, on 7 March 413, he was assassinated in Carthage, his supporters killed, his consulship revoked and his property confiscated by Constantius.[77] For the first time since 407 the Western Roman Empire was free from usurpations and internal warfare, simply needing time to restore order and repair the damage in large parts of Gaul, Italy and Africa. Constantius would use the property and wealth confiscated from Heraclianus' estate to pay for his consulship in 414, but would be disappointed by the limited funds the estate was to provide.[78]

On the other hand, Heraclianus' revolt immediately had a major impact upon affairs in Europe. Due to the embargo from Africa, Honorius could not supply food to the Goths. Yet due to the fact that an agreement had been reached and the Goths were now seen as allies of the regime in Ravenna, Athaulf and his men were granted entry into Narbonne and Toulouse.[79] Despite the 'loss' of these cities, the regime in Ravenna probably had great hopes for the future: due to the elimination of usurpers, Honorius and Constantius could now focus all their attention upon the Goths and the re-establishment of the West.

Chapter Seven

The Gothic Wars

413

While attention in Ravenna remained focused on the Goths, in Gaul the Franks expanded their territory around Trier, probably by a peaceful expansion of settlement rather than extensive military activity. The usurpations and invasions in Gaul had seriously disjointed the Roman military machine and the Franks and other barbarians along the frontier north of the newly-settled Burgundians would have been free to act.

Recognizing the weakness of his position should the Romans manage to continually isolate him without food, Athaulf also dispatched troops to capture nearby cities and their cache of supplies. Pretending to agree to the terms proposed by Honorius, Athaulf chose Marseille as his main target, hoping to take it 'by treachery'.[1] The citizens refused to allow him entry and an attempt to storm the town was defeated and Athaulf himself wounded by *comes* Boniface, a man who would have a major impact upon later imperial history.[2] Athaulf retreated to Narbonne to consider his next move and recover from his wound.

It may be that the continued attempts of Athaulf to force Honorius to agree peace on his own terms may have resulted in another attempt by Honorius to recruit new troops: in either late 412 or early 413 the writer Olympius was sent on a mission to the Huns. Sadly, Olympius does not record the details of his mission, so it is impossible to say whether it was aimed at recruiting troops, or even whether it was sent by the Eastern or Western courts.[3]

414

Nominated in 413, on 1 January 414 Constantius celebrated his consulship, using the profits from Heraclianus' estates in Africa to pay for the elaborate ceremonies surrounding his elevation.[4] Although his

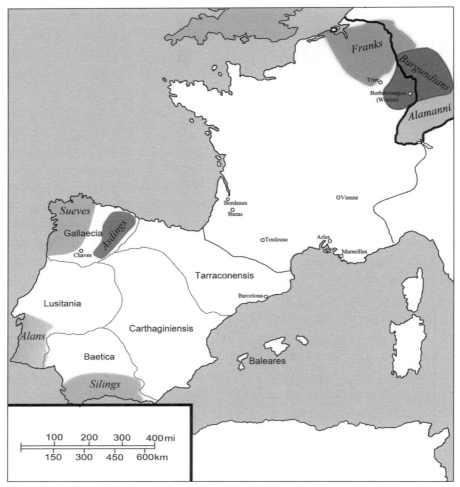

Map 9: The Gothic War in Gaul and Hispania.

rise was continuing and affairs in Italy were becoming stable, in Gaul confusion, invasion and famine continued.

While Constantius was preparing to celebrate his consulship, in Gaul in late 413 Athaulf still needed extra supplies of food, largely thanks to the ongoing famine but also because the grain promised by Honorius had not materialized due to Heraclianus' revolt. However, Honorius still swore to deliver the grain when he could in return for the release of Galla Placidia.[5] In order to maintain the moral advantage, Athaulf demanded an increased amount of grain, so that when he then refused to hand over Galla Placidia he would be seen by his followers as being in the right.[6]

The subsequent refusal by Athaulf to return Galla Placidia resulted in Constantius increasing the military pressure on the Goths. In a blatant snub to the imperial regime, and also as a response to both the failure to supply grain plus the military pressure being applied by Constantius, on 1 January 414 Athaulf raised the stakes, marrying Galla Placidia.[7] An elaborate ceremony was held in Narbonne, with the wedding following Roman traditions and gifts being given that were part of the loot from the Sack of Rome. In addition, an *epithalamium* (a traditional wedding speech) was given by Attalus. The claim by Jordanes that the marriage took place at Forum Julii is mistaken.[8]

The marriage was obviously an attempt by Athaulf to insert himself into the imperial hierarchy, possibly in imitation of the example set by Stilicho, although Stilicho was always a part of the social and military structure. The later claim that Athaulf had stated that he had changed his mind and now wanted to defend 'Romania' rather than replace it with 'Gothia' is most likely simply a story to excuse Galla Placidia's acceptance of Athaulf as her husband.[9]

If Athaulf had hoped to be acknowledged as part of the imperial regime with the marriage, he was to be sorely disappointed. Obviously Honorius and the court at Ravenna were horrified at the thought of an imperial princess being married to a 'barbarian', plus it was now becoming clear that Constantius himself had plans to marry Placidia, so ensuring his entry into the imperial family in the way that his predecessor Stilicho had done.

Furthermore, there was little chance of the Eastern regime in Constantinople accepting such a marriage. In December 414 the busts of Honorius, the Eastern emperor Theodosius and Theodosius' sister Pulcheria were displayed in Constantinople. The fact that Placidia was omitted suggests that her marriage to Athaulf had resulted in her being cast from the imperial lineage, as otherwise her soon-to-be-born son Theodosius, half-Goth and half-Roman, could be seen as an heir.[10]

Perhaps shortly after the marriage ceremony, and with the approval of many Gauls – most likely those that had earlier thrown their support behind Constantine III and Jovinus in opposition to the regime in Ravenna – the Goths may have been allowed to enter other cities and towns in Gaul, although the only town attested in the sources is Bordeaux.[11]

As a consequence of their attempt to establish themselves in Gaul with some Gallic help, plus the obvious affront of Athaulf marrying Galla Placidia, Constantius began to exert military pressure on the Goths, sending ships to begin a naval blockade of Narbonne and being 'allocated' troops by Honorius to recover Placidia by force, with the campaign being launched from Arles.[12] The immediate response of Athaulf was to declare Attalus emperor in Bordeaux.[13]

The weakness of Athaulf's position with regard to Honorius and Constantius was now clear to all. Repulsed from Marseille, he was forced by Constantius' blockade to abandon Narbonne after sacking the city, retreating to Bordeaux.[14] In Bordeaux, Attalus, once more a 'Gothic' emperor, appointed a man named Paulinus as his *Comes privatae largitionis* (Count of the Sacred Largesse). It is this man's testimony that allows a theoretical reconstruction of events.

Shortly after his retreat to Bordeaux, Athaulf finally realized that he could not defeat Constantius as the Romans had the benefit of a sophisticated logistical system which could keep the army fed despite the ongoing famine in Gaul; Athaulf had no such luxury. He took the decision to abandon Gaul and attempt to cross the Pyrenees into Hispania.[15]

Athaulf gathered his troops and headed south, leaving Attalus (and Paulinus) behind. Attalus was quickly captured and sent to Italy.[16] The Goths set fire to Bordeaux as they left, while Paulinus' house was looted and destroyed and he too decided to leave. On the way south, he came to Bazas, where a mixed force of Goths and Alans was laying siege to the town. Neither the commander of the Goths nor of the Alans is named in the sources. It is possible that this was the main army led by Athaulf, but if so it is strange that his 'defeat' in the siege is not mentioned in the sources. On the other hand, it is likely that the Alans were led by Goar. He had crossed into Gaul in 406 and quickly allied his men with the Romans, probably joining them to the forces led by Constantine III. Consequently, in 411, with the defeat of Constantine imminent, he had joined with the Burgundians in elevating Jovinus as usurper. With the defeat of Jovinus at the hands of Athaulf, Goar appears to have aligned with Athaulf. Consequently, as a man capable of changing allegiances when necessity demanded, it is likely that he was in command of the Alans at the Siege of Bazas.

Fortunately for Paulinus, he had previously formed a strong friendship with Goar (if indeed it was Goar). Determined to realign himself with the legitimate dynasty in Ravenna, Paulinus now convinced Goar to again switch allegiance, this time away from Athaulf. It may not have taken much to convince Goar that such a change was in his best interest. Goar allowed his wife and son to enter the town as hostages, before being allowed into the town to reinforce the garrison.[17] With the defenders now strengthened, the Goths raised the siege and continued on their way to the Pyrenees. By his actions Goar was able to ensure the survival of his men within the imperial system as the regime at Ravenna slowly regained control of Gaul.

Theodosius

In the meantime, the Goths continued their journey towards the Pyrenees. The new marriage was obviously one of mutual attraction: Placidia quickly bore a son, named Theodosius by his parents, either late in 414 or early in 415, when the Goths were either on their way to or already in Hispania.[18] The birth would have caused major consternation in Ravenna: Theodosius was the grandson of one emperor and first cousin to another. Moreover, and of far more importance, Theodosius was the nephew of Honorius and, as Honorius was childless, Theodosius could theoretically be in line to succeed.[19]

In the meantime, the Goths crossed the Pyrenees and took control of Barcelona.[20] Almost immediately, fortunately for Rome, but sadly for his parents, Theodosius died soon after reaching the city, being buried in a silver coffin outside the city walls.[21] The threat of having a half-Goth sitting on the imperial throne was removed.

It would appear that, with the 'victories' over the Goths and their subsequent flight to Hispania, Honorius granted the title of *patricius* to Constantius.[22] He had now achieved the same status as his predecessor Stilicho. The only move necessary to complete his rise was marriage into the imperial family. Stilicho had married his daughters to the emperor: Constantius was unmarried and had no children, so he was intent on marrying into the family in person. For this, he needed Galla Placidia to be freed from Gothic 'captivity' in order to marry her himself. This appears to have been part of his strategy from the start, which was why he had constantly encouraged Honorius to reject all Athaulf's peace overtures unless Placidia was released.[23] However, far from recovering Placidia, she was taken over the Pyrenees into Hispania with her husband and the rest of the Goths.

Meanwhile, in Gaul, it would appear that Honorius was forced into recognizing the presence of the Burgundians within imperial territory: with the ongoing war against the Goths, Honorius needed a stable northern frontier in Gaul that would not siphon troops away from the most important campaign.[24]

Hispania[25]

In Hispania, the Alans, Vandals and Sueves had long settled into their respective regions. Although it is dangerous to argue a point from lack of evidence, especially in eras where data is scarce, it is interesting that there is no reference in any of the sources to them attempting to either raid the neighbouring regions or expand their allotted territory. It would appear that for the first years of their settlement the Alans, Vandals and Sueves were intent upon settling their families on lands capable of supporting themselves.

Hydatius suggests that the Alans were the 'overlords' of the Vandals and the Sueves; however, this may simply be a matter of geography, with the Alans being in the centre, between the Silings to the south and the Asdings and Sueves to the north. In addition, they appear to have had close connections with the local Roman leaders, an impression reinforced by the economic evidence, which suggests that the territory ruled by the Alans retained strong economic ties with the Empire, as well as retaining a strong economy.[26]

Although, as noted above, there is no specific evidence confirming a treaty between the Empire and the non-Romans in Hispania, the fact that Orosius implies that they tried to come to an agreement with Rome and the subsequent lack of any military activity suggests that an informal agreement was reached, possibly in 411 after the defeat of Gerontius.[27] That does not mean, however, that Honorius had accepted their presence in Hispania; simply that between 409 and the entry of the Goths into Hispania there were enemies within the Empire who had a far higher priority, so peace in Hispania was imperative.[28] However, they were still harbouring the usurper Maximus who, following the defeat of Gerontius, had fled to them for safety, and since then they would appear to have refused to return him to the Empire.[29] For Honorius and Constantius the continued existence of a usurper, even though he was now inactive, was unfinished business that needed a conclusion at some point in the future.

If Athaulf had hoped that crossing into Hispania would relieve the Roman pressure on the Goths, he was to be disappointed: Constantius maintained the embargo as the Goths crossed the Pyrenees, most likely by shadowing the Gothic march and attacking any foraging parties rash enough to stray too far from the main body. Although Athaulf managed to take control of the city of Barcelona, relieving some of his supply difficulties for a short period of time, the continuing blockade by both land and sea ensured that his people remained undersupplied with food, a problem exacerbated by the fact that, like Gaul, Hispania was undergoing something of a famine. Still, the Goths were now in a region less damaged by barbarian invasions and usurpations than Gaul, so Athaulf may have held high hopes for an upturn in the Goths' fortunes.

Events after the Goths' arrival in Hispania are shrouded in mystery, especially due to the confusion inherent in the sources concerning what happened and when, so it is difficult to establish a clear and concise chronology. What follows is an attempt to outline a probable course of events which allows as much of the information as possible to be used.

Hydatius

The main source for this period is Hydatius. Hydatius later became bishop of Aquae Flaviae (probably modern-day Chaves) in Gallaecia. During his lifetime this region had been taken by the invading Sueves and Asding Vandals and as a consequence his chronicle is heavily flavoured by his contacts with the barbarians in the region. His *Chronicle* is a major source for this period and as such has been heavily studied. The main criticism concerning the *Chronicle* is the 'inaccurate chronology' that can be found throughout, and this has led many to question the accuracy of the whole work.

However, the majority of this criticism is based on an uncritical assessment of the circumstances surrounding the compilation of the chronicle, mainly due to modern authorities basing their valuation upon modern expectations and communication methods. The main criticism concerns his reporting of the wider world. However, as he was dependent upon travellers and merchants for the relaying of distant news, which by the time it arrived in Hispania was usually out of date, it is more likely their reports that were inaccurate: Hydatius simply had no means of checking the accuracy of their information and so simply inserted what he was told in his chronology at the reported date, or used 'informed guesswork'. Of more concern for those studying events in Hispania, although when writing about local events Hydatius is usually accepted as being relatively accurate, sometimes events are inverted or simply in the wrong place. An example of this which impacts on evaluation of the Goths in Hispania concerns his entry for 416:

> Athaulf, forced by *patricius* Constantius to abandon Narbona and make for Spain, was murdered in Barcelona by a certain Goth during an intimate conversation. He was succeeded as king by Vallia, who soon made peace with *patricius* Constantius and then turned against the Alans and Siling Vandals, who were settled in Lusitania and Baetica.
>
> *Hydatius 52[60] (a.416), trans. Burgess.*

According to modern practice, in theory this entry attests that soon after his accession in 416 Wallia led his army against the Alans and Vandals. However, it is a recurrent feature in contemporary chronicles to have snippets of information concerning later events placed in an earlier entry, whether for clarity concerning links to later events or to heighten the tension for the reader. In this case, it would appear that Hydatius is not necessarily attesting to an early attack, instead linking the newly-crowned Wallia with the major events which were to follow.

In addition, it is usually assumed that Hydatius – and others – were attempting to list events not solely by year, but by chronological narratives within the year. This may indeed be possible. However, it is also feasible that events were written either as the writer remembered them or in order of importance. It is also feasible that, as these works were compiled over a length of time, the exact method changed as the author aged.

Taking this analysis into account, it is here assumed that Hydatius' chronology is tolerably accurate for the local events in Hispania and consequently other sources are used either for confirmation or for additional detail. Furthermore, as it is not accepted as fact that Hydatius placed things in an exact chronological order, each analyzed entry will, where necessary, be assessed upon its own merits.

Athaulf

By crossing the Pyrenees, Athaulf had evaded the immediate attention of the Roman army, as Constantius would need time to organize a similar blockade in Hispania where his control and military presence were doubtless still low. However, Athaulf now came into close contact with two of the tribes that had earlier entered the peninsula. Desperate for food after their travels, the Goths began to buy supplies from the Alans and the Siling Vandals: it is unlikely that the Asdings or the Sueves were involved in these exchanges due in part to the long distances involved but mainly to the lack of surplus food (due to the ongoing famine) being available for trade in the poorer arable regions of Gallaecia. In particular, the Vandals and the Goths had a long-standing animosity going back through the centuries and, displaying a distinct lack of common sense, the Siling traders began to mock the hungry and desperate Goths, calling them

> *Truli* because when they were oppressed by hunger they bought grain from the Vandals at one *solidus* per *trula*. A *trula* is one-third of a *sextarius*.[30]
>
> *Olympiodorus fragment 29.1.*

Translations of the Latin words *trula* and *truli* have differed, but perhaps the most accurate in the modern sense of *trula* is 'spoonful': in effect, the Vandals were calling the Goths 'spoonies', a strange nickname but one indicative of the Goths' desperate plight.[31]

Although their travels and the lengthy blockade had weakened the Goths, they were still a force to be reckoned with: according to Jordanes, Athaulf, having established his capital at Barcelona, left his treasure and the unfit in the city and led the army against the Vandals. Sadly, though, Jordanes does not include any details concerning the nature of either the outbreak or the course of the conflict.[32]

It is likely that Athaulf simply led a swift campaign against the Vandals, raiding their settlements and taking all the supplies they could find. However, this was merely a punitive expedition. Athaulf could not embark upon a major campaign: obviously, the Goths' treasure and families in Barcelona were vulnerable to attack from Constantius when the army was absent. Furthermore, the supplies taken were needed in Barcelona, so a swift return was necessary. It may be as a consequence of this outbreak of war in Hispania that the Vandals, Sueves and Alans in Hispania sent a message to Honorius stating that the campaigns against the Goths were going well; an attempt to further ingratiate themselves with the regime in Ravenna.[33]

On the other hand, with the attack the Goths had lost connection with one of their major suppliers of food. Many Goths appear to have been losing their faith in Athaulf's ability to feed them or find them a secure place to settle: after all, they had been wandering the Empire for seven years and were still no nearer being able to settle and live 'normal' lives. At this point affairs took an unexpected twist. Athaulf was assassinated, according to Jordanes by one 'Euervulf, a man whose short stature he had been wont to mock', according to Olympiodorus by a man named Dubius, one of Sarus' followers.[34] Given subsequent events, it would appear that the latter is more likely.

In short order Placidia had to face the loss of the two closest men in her life. As noted above, shortly after their arrival in Hispania and entry into Barcelona, her son Theodosius had died, and now her husband was dead. Instantly, her future among the Goths had become extremely precarious.

Segeric

Immediately following the death of Athaulf a man named Segeric was elected as king. According to Olympiodorus, Segeric was the brother of Sarus, who had earlier been killed by Athaulf in Gaul.[35] When all the evidence is analyzed, the most likely course of events is that dissatisfaction concerning Athaulf's leadership had grown and an opposition group had focused upon Sarus' brother Segeric, with Sarus' retainer Dubius being the man chosen as the assassin due to his being in close contact with Athaulf.

If the above is accurate, the fact that Segeric was made king is slightly surprising: there had obviously been a strong antipathy between Athaulf and Sarus, so the possibility that Athaulf and Segeric had co-existed is odd. The most likely explanation is that Sarus and Segeric were estranged, and that Segeric simply used his family connection in order to promote his own political standing within the Gothic hierarchy.

The latter concept is reinforced by subsequent events. According to Orosius, Segeric was perceived by many among the Goths as being too willing to accede to Roman demands and accept a treaty that would ensure the subservience of the Goths to Roman rule, but other factors suggest that this is a later invention.[36] In fact, Segeric may have been the figurehead for an extremist faction within the Gothic polity who were unwilling to accept a treaty with Rome in any circumstances. In this context, his treatment of Placidia becomes easier to understand. Placidia was forced to walk with the captives, followed by a mounted Sigeric. Sigeric was demonstrating to all that he was against a Roman treaty: by denigrating Placidia in a manner which Honorius would hear about, he enhanced his image of being an opponent of surrendering to Rome.

Segeric's attempt at enhancing his popularity failed: by this stage the majority of the Goths may simply have wanted peace with the Empire and land on which to support themselves. Segeric quickly became unpopular and within only seven days he too was assassinated.[37] After a short delay the Goths elevated a new man to be their leader. He is not attested as being related to any earlier leaders of the Goths, and his subsequent policy suggests that he was in the opposite political camp to Segeric. His name was Wallia.[38]

Chapter Eight

The Gothic Wars in Hispania

Athaulf was dead. His immediate successor Segeric was dead. Wallia, the new king, found himself in a tricky situation. It was obvious that there was a strong faction opposed to any dealings with Rome, but there appears to have been an equally strong group that wished for an end to their sufferings and wanderings and who simply wanted a secure home; whether this was in alliance with Rome or not was immaterial.

It would appear that, realizing that there was to be no peaceful settlement in Hispania, Wallia attempted to cross back into Gaul, where at least some of the inhabitants were opposed to the rule of Honorius and Constantius. The *Gallic Chronicle of 452* records an attempt to cross back into Gaul that was repulsed by the army, led by Constantius.[1]

Balked in their attempt to cross the Pyrenees, at least some of the Goths again attempted to cross to Africa. What actually happened is unclear due to a discrepancy in the sources. According to Orosius, it was just one group of Goths who either commandeered or rented some boats in an attempt to sail to Africa.[2] However, it has been assumed by some that the attempt was made under the auspices of Wallia himself.[3] Whatever the case, the attempt failed: the ships sank and it became clear to all that, at least for the moment, Africa was beyond the reach of the Goths.

Assessing his options, Wallia was forced to accept that with the continuing food shortages, plus the failed attempts at reaching either Gaul or Africa and an ongoing conflict with the Siling Vandals (and possibly also with the Alans) in Hispania, a treaty with Rome was the only option left open to him.[4] Probably in late 415 the Vandals opened talks with Rome, Constantius sending Euplutius, an *agens in rebus*, to negotiate on his behalf.[5]

416

The winter of 415–416 was almost certainly the happiest at the court in Ravenna since before the death of Stilicho in 408. All the usurpers were either dead (Constantine III, Jovinus, Heraclianus) or at least completely removed from power (Attalus, Maximus). In fact, when Honorius celebrated a triumph at Rome in 416 he was able to display the captured Attalus before having him mutilated and exiled to the island of Lipara.[6]

Furthermore, with the ongoing negotiations with Wallia being made from a position of strength, it could be expected that the Goths would accede to the Roman demands and accept their subordinate status. In addition, with the repulse of the Goths' attempt to re-cross the Pyrenees, it was now safe to assume that the Empire was in a position to pacify Gaul and reintegrate it into the Empire. Recognizing that steps were needed to ensure that no further uprisings would take place north of the Pyrenees, in 416 the government lightened the taxes in Gaul.[7]

In the meantime, negotiations with Wallia finally managed to hammer out an agreement that would allow the Empire to recover from the havoc caused by the Goths in Italy and Gaul.[8]

Unfortunately, the exact details of the agreement are not described by the sources and, of equal importance, the chronology of events between 416 and 419 is unclear as the sources are often contradictory, making certainty impossible. Consequently, what follows is hypothesis based upon all the sources and as such it should be noted that the chronology and analysis of this sequence of events may change due to either new findings or new interpretations.

The Gothic Treaty of 416

It is usually assumed that in 416 a treaty was signed between Rome and Wallia in which Wallia released Galla Placidia, exchanged hostages, received supplies and arranged for a Gothic settlement in southern Gaul and for the Goths to serve as *foederati*.[9] However, it has also been suggested that in this treaty the Goths were not to be *settled* as *foederati*, agreeing only to supply men to serve in the Roman army under the *foedus* (treaty).[10] A close analysis of the sources suggests that all these hypotheses may be too simplistic, as other events – especially in Hispania – imply a far greater complexity than is usually accepted.

Instead, it may be more accurate to suggest that in 416 the Goths were in no position to request that they be given land as part of the treaty. Although many of the Goths in Wallia's army were seasoned warriors who may in fact have been among those who had entered Italy under Radagaisus, and who had an unremitting hatred of Rome due to their families having been slaughtered after Stilicho's execution, they were in no position to make demands upon Honorius and Constantius. At this stage they were living under constant embargo and were desperate for food. In view of earlier examples of such treaties, for example that of the Goths under Radagaisus in 406, it would be expected that the Goths would be dispersed around the Western Empire, with many of the men of military age agreeing to serve in the Roman army. Instead, it is here assumed that, after an initial round of talks, the Goths agreed to return Placidia and give hostages in return for a supply of 600,000 measures (probably *modii*) of grain.[11] There was, as yet, no mention of either settlement or of attacking the tribes in Hispania. This proposition would help to explain the confusion concerning other events that are attested as happening in Hispania at this time. It would also suit Constantius' attested agenda: more than anything, he needed Placidia to return in order for him to marry her and so secure his position within the imperial hierarchy.

This simple agreement might receive some support from the alleged nature of the meeting: according to Jordanes, the treaty may have been arranged at a pass in the Pyrenees, probably immediately after the repulse of Wallia's attempt to return to Gaul, although the nature of Jordanes' account at this point makes this theory uncertain.[12]

The first of the other events noted above is an oft-overlooked brief entry in Hydatius:

Vallia…soon made peace with *patricius* Constantius and then turned against the Alans and Siling Vandals, who were settled in Lusitania and Baetica.

Hydatius 22 (52[60]), trans. Burgess.

The fact that this attack is not yet associated with a treaty with Rome implies that it was not undertaken under Roman auspices. Although only attested by Hydatius, such an attack is likely to have taken place: in 415 Athaulf had attacked the two tribes and so it is probable that the

Alans and/or Silings had launched retaliatory raids against the Goths, especially those separating from the main body to forage. Accordingly, after receiving the grain from Constantius, Wallia attacked in response to unrecorded Alan and Vandal raids. It may be this event that is alluded to by Orosius when he looked forward to the elimination of the Vandals and Sueves in Hispania by a combination of Rome and the Goths.[13]

Again the sources do not provide any clarification, but if the above hypothesis is in any way accurate, these attacks and counter-attacks help to explain a further piece of information contained in the *Gallic Chronicle of 452*: in 416 Maximus, the man who had been elevated as emperor by Gaudentius in Hispania in 409 and who had fled to the barbarians following Gaudentius' defeat in 411, again laid claim to the title of *Augustus*.[14]

Possibly the only explanation for his sudden reappearance is that, learning of the peace treaty between the Goths and Rome, the Siling Vandals and the Alans assumed that Wallia's attack was under the instigation of the Empire rather than being simply a response to raids from their own tribesmen. Therefore, in emulation of the Goths in Italy with Attalus and the Burgundians on the Rhine with Jovinus, the Alans and Silings nominated their own man as emperor. The Empire once again had a usurper at large in the West.

This hypothesis also explains why Rome was soon to turn the Goths upon the Siling Vandals and the Alans. Prior to this, there does not appear to be any reason for Honorius or Constantius to declare war upon the Alans and Vandals. The Alans, the Siling Vandals, the Asding Vandals and the Sueves had been quiet in Hispania from at least 411 following the death of Gerontius, and although the animosity between the Goths and the Vandals had created tension in Hispania, there was no real reason for Rome to wish to begin yet another conflict. With the 'elevation' of Maximus, the Alans and the Silings signalled their split from Rome and their intention to oppose Honorius.[15] Obviously, if at all possible, the Empire would need to react.

The fact that the Goths were already at war with the Alans and Vandals meant that Rome did not have to convince Wallia that they were the common enemy. As an added bonus, the infighting between the barbarians would weaken all three of these opponents while leaving the Roman army untouched. Honorius and Constantius were in effect using one barbarian nation to eliminate two others, with no inherent downside for Rome: Roman troops would not be involved in the fighting, it would free Constantius and the army to pursue other goals, and the only 'losses' would be the need to continue to supply the Goths during their campaigns.

Yet although the Alans and Silings had become the common enemy, Constantius may have needed to add an incentive to convince the

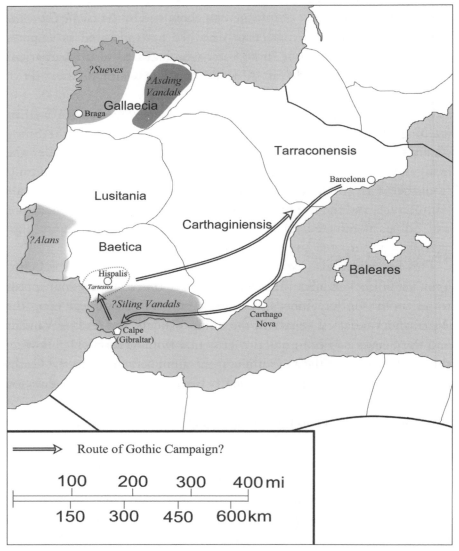

Map 10: The proposed Gothic campaign against the Vandals and Alans.

Goths to launch a major campaign in Hispania, either with or without Roman military support. In this context, it would appear that Wallia and Constantius were involved in an ongoing series of negotiations that would constantly realign the two sides throughout the period 416–418, a factor that may in part explain the confusion in both ancient and modern sources, who expect there to be a single defining treaty signed at one point in time. Consequently, it is possible to suggest that over the winter of 416–417 Constantius and Wallia engaged in further talks during which it was agreed that the Goths would campaign against Maximus and his supporters in return for a continuous supply of grain and other necessities. It may also be during these negotiations that an agreement was reached in which the Goths would be allowed to settle in Gaul but, if the above hypothesis that there were continuous talks between Constantius and Wallia is true, it may be more likely that at this early stage Constantius was not contemplating a permanent Gothic settlement in Gaul. He may simply have been working on a day-to-day basis rather than having a long-term strategy, using the Goths to weaken the Alans and Silings to the point where the Empire could deal with them in person, a long-standing Roman practice of using barbarians to attack barbarians.

The Gothic Campaigns

The sources concerning the nature and the course of the campaigns waged by the Goths against the Alans and the Silings are confusing and slightly contradictory, especially with regard to the dating. The outline presented here is based around that contained in Hydatius' chronicle, since he was alive at the time and writing about contemporary events. In addition, living in Hispania, it is here assumed that his chronology is the most accurate when analyzing events in Hispania.

It is worthwhile at this point to analyze the text of Hydatius' chronicle to fully understand his account:

Wallia, rex Gothorum, Romani nominis causa intra Hispanias caedes magnas efficit barbarorum.

In the name of Rome Wallia, the king of the Goths, inflicted a vast slaughter upon the barbarians in Spain.

Hydatius 23 (55[63]) a. 417, trans. Burgess.

Sadly, this is the only mention of a campaign in 417, and consequently it has been seen by some as a duplication, either by Hydatius himself or by one of the later copiers. Assuming that Hydatius is neither confused nor miscopied, it would appear that in 417 Wallia led a restricted campaign against the Alans and the Vandals, either winning a battle or, more likely, conducting a heavy raid into the lands of the Alans, killing many, taking captives and sacking settlements. The speed at which the campaign was launched may account for it being of a limited scale in either size or duration or both. In addition, Wallia may have been wary of Constantius' intentions and so have left many men behind to guard the Goths' families against potential Roman treachery.

However, at roughly the same time Exuperantius was leading a campaign to recover control of Armorica. Consequently, it may have only been when on campaign that Wallia learned of Exuperantius' campaign in Armorica and have realized that Constantius was going to be true to his word. With this 'proof' of good faith, Wallia may have been prepared to lead a larger attack on the Alans and Vandals in the following year, on condition that Constantius continued to implement his part of the treaty.

The Gothic Campaign of 418[16]

As a consequence of this analysis, it would appear that both Athaulf and Wallia had led campaigns against the Alans and Silings prior to a full agreement being reached with Rome. However, because Maximus had again raised the standard of revolt using the barbarians in Hispania as his military arm, it is likely that in either late 417 or early 418 Constantius and Wallia reached a new supplementary agreement. In this treaty, the Goths would be given land to settle in return for them waging a major campaign against the Alans and Silings, but this time with imperial logistical support.

With Constantius beginning the necessary arrangements for the Gothic settlement over the winter of 417–418, Wallia made the preparations for a renewed conflict. Due to the elevation of Maximus, it is possible that on this campaign Wallia was supported by troops under the *Comes Hispaniae* Sabinianus.[17] The added presence of Roman allies may have given Wallia the confidence to take the majority of his forces against the Siling Vandals and the Alans, which would help to explain the devastation described by Hydatius. Again, it is necessary to analyze Hydatius' comments to understand what happened:

Solis facta defectio die decimo quarto kal. Augusti, qui fuit quinta feria.

There was an eclipse of the sun on [19 July 418], which was a Thursday.

Durante episcopo quo supra, gravissimo terraemotu sancta in Hierosolymis loca quassantur.

While the aforementioned bishop was still in office, the holy places in Jerusalem were shaken by a terrible earthquake.

Wandali Silingi in Baetica per Walliam regem omnes exstincti.

All of the Siling Vandals in Baetica were wiped out by King Wallia.

Alani qui Wandalis et Suevis potentabantur, adeo caesi sunt a Gothis, ut exstincto Atace [Addace] *rege ipsorum, pauci qui superfuerant, abolito regni nomine, Gunderici, regis Wandalorum, qui in Gallaecia resederat, se patrocinio subjugarent.*

The Alans, who were ruling over the Vandals and Sueves, suffered such heavy losses at the hands of the Goths that after the death of their King, Addax, the few survivors, with no thought of their own kingdom, placed themselves under the protection of Gunderic, the king of the Vandals, who had settled in Gallaecia.

Gothi intermisso certamine quod agebant, per Constantium ad Gallias revocati, sedes in Aquitanica a Tolosa usque ad Oceanum acceperunt.

The Goths broke off the campaign which they were waging and were recalled by Constantius to Gaul where they were given settlements in Aquitania from Tolosa [Toulouse] all the way to the Ocean.

Hydatius 23–24 (58–61[66–69]), a. 418, trans. Burgess.

Dealing with the initial two entries first, these have sometimes been used to demonstrate that Hydatius' chronicle was inaccurate. The earthquake in Jerusalem is actually dated to 419, and so it has been suggested that

Hydatius may have been out by a year either way in his dating. However, the solar eclipse actually passed over Hispania and so was dated accurately. Consequently, as noted earlier, it is here assumed that Hydatius' entries are accurate when dealing with events in Hispania, and it is only with entries reported long after the event elsewhere in the Empire that Hydatius' sources may have inaccurately recalled the date.

Having decided that Hydatius' dating for the campaigns is accurate, it is then necessary to analyze the next two entries. In these, Hydatius appears to record two separate campaigns: the first against the Vandals in Baetica, and the second against the Alans in Lusitania.

Supporting Hydatius' narrative is a passage from Sidonius Apollinaris' panegyric to the emperor Anthemius. Although given much later in 468, it mentions the deeds of the ancestors of the *patricius* Ricimer, often seen as the power behind Anthemius' throne. Among these ancestors Sidonius names Wallia, king of the Goths:[18] 'Wallia, [Ricimer's] grandfather, defeated the Vandal hordes and the Alans, their allies in war, in Tartessian lands, and their bodies covered Calpe, in the West.'[19]

In theory, this extract not only supports the concept of there being either two distinct campaigns or of one campaign with two objectives, but it also gives some extra detail. On the other hand, as this is a panegyric written half a century after the event, there is no guarantee about Sidonius' accuracy. Nevertheless, with few other references to work from, it is accepted here as being (relatively) accurate.

One aspect of Sidonius' work is that it reinforces the concept that the Silings and the Alans were allied, though it is interesting to note that Sidonius does not claim that the Alans were the senior partner in the alliance. Interestingly, Sidonius mentions neither the Asding Vandals nor the Sueves: it is probable that the only alliance was between the Silings and the Asdings, and that the Asdings and the Sueves were not part of the alliance and, being weak, were of little interest to Rome. This hypothesis contradicts the generally accepted theory that the four barbarian tribes in Hispania were mutually supportive and retained the enmity of the Goths and the Romans. Moreover, the proposition implies that Maximus was proclaimed emperor only by the Silings and the Alans, and that the Asdings and the Sueves were not immediately involved in the usurpation.

Possibly of more importance, Sidonius claims that there was a battle in 'Tartessian lands' and that the 'bodies covered Calpe'. 'Tartessos' is the ancient term for the region around the mouth of the River Guadalquivir, whereas 'Calpe' is either situated on the eastern coast of Hispania (Calp) or, and possibly more likely, the ancient name for Gibraltar, which assumption is made here. Both of these terms are archaic, used more to display Sidonius' literary abilities than being an exact location for a battle, but they may still be of some use in assessing the nature of the campaign. Consequently, the following hypothesis allows a logical description of the campaign, but it should be remembered that it is only hypothesis and that new finds or new interpretations may alter it.

In early 418, and acting with the support of Rome, Wallia led his army on a devastating attack on the Silings. Since the Silings were settled in Baetica, in southern Hispania, it makes sense to assume that the route of the attack followed the coastline, allowing Constantius to supply the Goths by sea, and even directly from Africa if that was deemed necessary. Of equal importance, by using the coastal roads the Goths may have been able to reach Siling-held territory without the Silings receiving advance notice. Surprised, the Silings retreated towards the south and sent a request for support to the Alans. The advance was so swift that the Alans were unable to gather their forces and march to the support of their allies in time, hence Hydatius' chronicle depicting the defeats of the Silings and the Alans in separate entries.

Moving inland from the coast and penetrating deep into the lands settled by the Silings, the Goths were able to devastate the majority of the Siling settlements and may even have defeated the Silings in pitched battle near Gibraltar, but if so no description or notice of its location survives. The assault was so devastating that Hydatius was able to report that 'All of the Siling Vandals in Baetica were wiped out by King Wallia.'

Having decimated the Silings with either minimal or no losses, Wallia prepared to turn his army north and head for the Alans in Lusitania. It is likely that, as he turned north, Wallia was met by the Alan army heading south to support the Silings, possibly near Tartessos. Hydatius writes that

The Alans, who were ruling over the Vandals and Sueves, suffered such heavy losses at the hands of the Goths that after the death of their King, Addax, the few survivors, with no thought of their own kingdom, placed themselves under the protection of Gunderic, the king of the Vandals, who had settled in Gallaecia.

It would appear that Wallia defeated the Alans and killed their king before going on to ravage their territory, causing massive losses to the Alans. As a consequence of this devastating campaign, the remnants of both the Alans and the Silings sought refuge with Gunderic in Gallaecia. It would appear that the usurper Maximus also fled to Gallaecia. In effect, the Goths had brought Baetica and Lusitania back within the Empire. However, by turning north, Wallia had lost access to Roman supplies.

It is usually claimed that the Goths were now 'recalled' by Constantius, rather than being forced to retire due to supply difficulties. In this hypothesis, the Roman government was worried that the Goths were becoming too powerful in Hispania and may have decided to ignore the treaty and founded instead an independent 'kingdom' in the peninsula. To some extent this may be true, but that would not fully explain the recall of the Goths. Instead, it is here assumed that the Goths retired on their own initiative due to losing their supply lines, and that the fears of the Roman government, coupled with the timetable for the upcoming Gothic settlement, meant that the Goths were not deployed against the Asdings and the Sueves in 419. Instead, attention focused almost solely on settling the Goths in Gaul.

Chapter Nine

The Gothic Settlement of 418–419[1]

The Terms

The treaty by which the Visigoths were settled in Aquitania and surrounding areas in 418 has been the subject of much debate, not helped by the fact that the Romans 'traditionally like[d] to hide diversity behind as few legal procedures as possible'.[2] In addition, it is often compared to the earlier attempts by Alaric to agree a settlement, especially those between 407 and 410, and in many respects it is similar to these.[3] The Goths were, at last, settled on land inside the Empire. However, although Wallia was accepted as the sole ruler of the Goths, much like Alaric, he was unable to accomplish Alaric's desire for a permanent, senior military post within the Roman hierarchy. Yet the treaty did acknowledge that the Goths were a separate political entity within the Empire and in many respects maintained their independence when settled.[4] It may have been hoped that over time they would be assimilated, as other barbarians had been in the past, and analysis has proved that in many ways the Goths did assimilate. Modern studies have shown 'lexical references only to social and institutional military status':[5] linguistically at least, the Goths became Roman. Politically, however, they remained separate.

Even more divisive is the debate surrounding the nature of the settlement itself. The argument is based upon the ambiguous phrasing used in the sources, which can be interpreted to either mean that the Visigoths were allocated money and treated as soldiers, or that they were granted land and its associated revenues.[6] As a result, argument has tended to crystallize around these two options, with supporters arguing vociferously over their preferred choice.

The greatest difficulty concerning an appraisal of the nature of the settlement is that both of these options are viable and supported to some extent by the sources. The problem, therefore, is that as both options are viable, neither will ever receive exclusive backing from modern historians. Consequently, it is necessary to analyze both before reaching a conclusion.[7]

The first claim is that the Goths were settled as *foederati* (agreeing to supply troops as part of a treaty), using the traditional Roman method of billeting known as *hospitalitas*. In this, it was usual for the settlers to be quartered in cities in return for military service, receiving *annonae* (wages).[8] There is some later evidence for this, and so for some this is an acceptable conclusion.[9]

The second possibility is a system where, usually, incoming barbarians were settled on the land and were granted one-third of the income from it. This method is supported by Philostorgius, who writes specifically that the Visigoths were granted land to farm in return for supplying troops when required.[10] In this vision of the settlement there was no need for the Goths to receive *hospitalitas*: they were given land and a supply of seeds in order to begin the transformation from enemies to settled friends who could be taxed. In this hypothesis, it is notable that even the Empire was forced to accept that due to the hardships of their years fighting against Rome the Goths were in poor condition, since they seem to have been given a tax exemption in order to help them recover after the initial settlement.[11] The difficulty here is that, unlike both earlier and later settlements, the evidence from later sources suggests that at some point the Goths appear to have acquired two-thirds of the income of the forfeited territory, leaving only one-third in the hands of the Romans.[12] Nevertheless, this hypothesis has received support from some modern historians.

The confusion present in the sources means that neither proposition can be seen as solely valid. On the other hand, what is sometimes forgotten by modern authors is that the agreements formed both before and after that which settled the Goths were agreed in completely different circumstances, so comparisons may be faulty. Usually, on other occasions the enemy were defeated by a triumphant Roman army and the defeated tribesmen settled according to whichever system the emperor (or his military leaders) decided. With the Goths, although they were in dire straits, they had not been decisively defeated in battle, nor were the Romans in a position of complete supremacy. Therefore, it is possible that the treaty that settled the Goths in Aquitania was more complex than that agreed with any other hostile force, either before or after.

In this hypothesis, the Goths were not settled in a simple 'either/or' manner, but using a more complex system that took into account the needs of an emerging Gothic nobility who would want their superior social status to be acknowledged, alongside that of the vast majority of the people, who would simply need and be given land to farm.[13] Consequently, it is here assumed that there were at least three methods of settlement for the Goths.

Prior to the reign of Alaric, the Goths had been a conglomeration of peoples with loyalties mainly to local leaders. However, Alaric and his entourage had used Roman models of power to gain control of the whole people.[14] Seeing this new hierarchy as a reflection of their own, the Romans may have given either large landed estates to the new Gothic higher aristocracy – land possibly taken from those who had supported the earlier usurpers – or they may have been given part-ownership of the country estates of (absentee) landlords, or something similar: this option may be represented in the sources by the term *sortes*.[15]

The lower orders may have been settled in a different manner, with 'smaller military units being settled on land under the household sovereignty of a military chief', which would later be expected to merge with the natives. This may have been a slight variation of the Roman system of *hospitalitas*, as this would mean that such men were immediately available for military service should the need arise, whether to serve the Gothic king or as allies of Rome. In addition, this may have been a preferred method of many Goths, the majority of whom 'identified more with local leaders than with the idea of a centralized monarchy'. During a migration there was a need for subordination to a single command, but for many Goths – and other peoples present in the 'Gothic' army – this would not be their preferred political choice, and as soon as possible loyalty to local leaders would once again become the norm.[16] This option may be represented in the sources by the term *sedes*.[17]

However, it is likely that the majority of the Goths, being families, were simply given land to farm. There appears to have been an abundance of *agri deserti* ('deserted lands': lands from which tax was no longer being produced, not necessarily lands abandoned or barren), as many of the land's proprietors had either died, fled or have had problems in finding the manpower to work their lands.[18] An alternative was *caduca* (land whose ownership had lapsed and the land had reverted to the fisc), or *res privatae* (imperial land). All of these may have been utilized to settle the Goths, theoretically resulting in them becoming self-sufficient farmers of potential future benefit to the Roman tax collectors.[19]

The concept that at least some of the Visigoths were granted land is reinforced by a review of the personalities involved in the treaty. Wallia was the leader of a large group of people who had been harassed out of Italy and forced, usually on the verge of starvation, along the southern coast of Gaul before being compelled to fight for the Empire in Hispania. There can be little doubt that the offer of land to farm for his people would have been accepted with a minimum of hesitation by Wallia.

On the part of the Romans, the *magister militum* Constantius had served under Theodosius I and had been a follower of Stilicho.[20] It is likely that Constantius used both the emperor and Stilicho as his military and political role models. As a result, Constantius followed the example set by Theodosius, settling the Goths in Gaul and imposing similar terms that Theodosius had applied in 382, although his weaker position may have resulted in concessions that would not have been dreamed of by Theodosius.

Although this solution may appear to be unnecessarily complex, it has the benefit of explaining the confusion in the ancient sources. These generally only attest to a singular explanation for most events, so both the ancient and the modern author are able to choose whichever of the two suits their narrative agenda. In addition, it helps to explain why Wallia was able to convince his people to accept the settlement. Wallia and his immediate supporters were granted exalted status and, although it was not at the level demanded by either Alaric or Athaulf, given the precarious position of the Goths after the deaths of the earlier kings, a position of influence in Gaul and the possibility of further promotion once accepted into the Roman hierarchy, would have given Wallia the leverage he needed to convince the nobles that the settlement was the best option. However, one outcome of the treaty was a division of interests between the Gothic aristocracy and their followers, with the nobility attempting to emulate the Roman aristocracy, whereas their followers now became the equivalent of Roman peasants.[21] Moreover, at no point were the Goths given official authority over native Romans.[22]

The complexity of the negotiations and the ensuing transfer of the Goths to their new homes may also explain the protracted nature of the treaty and of the settlement itself, with some dating the settlement to 418 and others to 419.[23] The complex nature of the distribution of the Goths to their new homes doubtless took a long time, with either individual Goths or Romans objecting to the new arrangements, meaning that the transfer began in 418 but the final touches were only instituted in 419.[24] If the above hypothesis is in any way accurate, then the negotiating skills of both Constantius and Wallia deserve recognition, as noted by at least one modern authority.[25]

Alongside the problem of the exact nature of the settlement itself is the difficulty of assessing whether or not the Goths agreed to supply troops to support the Roman army, usually as agreed in a *foedus* ('treaty', usually including the supply of troops in the terms). However, although

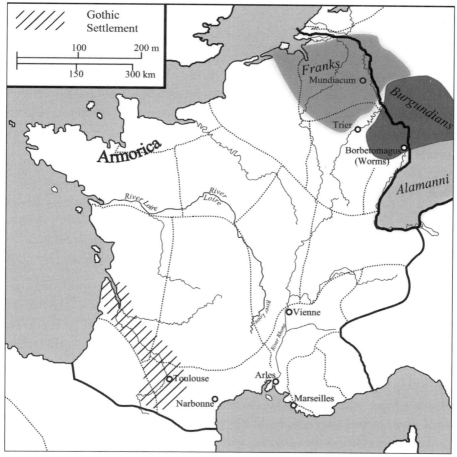

Map 11: The Gothic Settlement.

the Goths did later send troops to supplement Roman forces, the evidence is so fragmentary that it is impossible to say without doubt that a *foedus* had been agreed, although this is implied in the works of Sidonius Apollinaris.[26] However, if they actually had accepted the terms of a *foedus*, in reality such service was extremely intermittent and can be seen as unimportant: after the settlement the Goths disappear for long periods, 'as farmers are wont to do'.[27] Instead, it seems more likely that there was no such agreement, with the Romans instead being allowed to negotiate either with Wallia (or later Theodoric), or even with lower-level individual Gothic nobles, in order to recruit troops for specific campaigns.[28]

The Area Settled

The territory in which the Goths were settled was extensive, with the sources stating that it covered 'Aquitania II, Novempopulana and Narbonensis I from the Tyrrhenian Sea and the Rhone, along the Loire to the Atlantic'.[29] Although this would appear to be an extensive territory, the area settled is less than suggested. It appears to have stretched from the valley of the Garonne and Les Landes/Pyrenees in the south to just barely the Loire in the north.[30] This gave them much of Aquitania II, plus some cities in the neighbouring provinces of Novempopulana and Narbonensis; it did not give them all of these provinces.

Modern Assessment

It is common to find modern historians criticizing Theodosius, Constantius and their successors about their policy concerning the settlement of barbarians on Roman soil. The main problem addressed is that the new settlement, unlike those of earlier centuries in the West (although not in the East), retained their political leaders rather than being settled on Roman terms under Roman supervision and governed by Roman prefects.[31] This is alleged to be the first major flaw in the Roman plan: although the Goths were settled on land largely according to Roman terms, they remained a people apart with their own leader.

The second criticism of these settlements is due to the loss of revenue from the settled areas to a government whose coffers were already rapidly shrinking.[32] With the settlement of the Goths, these complaints reach their apogee. These theories tend to assume that all was well within the Empire, apart from the depredations of the Goths. Obviously this was not the case: Constantius needed to eliminate the Goths as a threat in order to concentrate his forces on other areas within the Empire that needed attention. Yet there remains the question of how Constantius came to his decisions concerning the Gothic problem.

Unable to evict the Goths, the decision to settle them in Gaul may still seem strange, given that Constantius' predecessor Stilicho had taken great pains to keep them out of the trans-Alpine region, yet it simply reflected political and strategic reality. At no point could the Romans have evicted the Goths from either Hispania or Gaul and forced them to return east without risking a major battle, hence a defeat on the scale of Adrianople in 378. Furthermore, the Western Empire did not have the surplus manpower for a campaign carried out in the teeth of fierce Gothic opposition: up to this point Constantius had used blockade rather than combat to limit the Goths' movements. Consequently, it is feasible to assume that the Goths would have resisted to their utmost any attempt to return them to their starting-point in Illyricum.

On the other hand, there were sensible, political reasons for settling the Goths in Gaul. Since the crossing of the Rhine by the barbarians in 406, conditions in Gaul had changed dramatically. By settling the Goths in Aquitania Constantius could set them to guard against any attempt by the surviving Vandals, Alans or Sueves to re-enter Gaul from Hispania. Moreover, they were now perfectly placed for campaigns against these tribes in Hispania should Constantius decide to attack again. In addition, although modern authors could expect there to be complaints against the settlement from local landowners, there may have been far fewer than expected. Against the loss of land to the incoming Goths must be set the fact that owners and landlords were still expected to pay tax on the unproductive land they were now to lose.[33] The lessening of taxes that they were struggling to pay needs to be offset against the lost but otherwise unproductive land.

In addition, although the strength of the Empire seemed to be reviving, affairs in Gaul were not yet settled. For example, despite the fact that Exuperantius had 'reconquered' Armorica, the natives in the region doubtless remained unhappy about imperial rule. Situated in Aquitania, not only were the Goths perfectly placed to intervene in Armorica should the inhabitants raise the standard of revolt and elevate yet another usurper, they were also in a position to support the nobles in and around the region they settled against further *bacaudic* rebellions, plus they could defend against any barbarian raids along the coast, giving the local aristocrats a further reason to acquiesce in the Gothic settlement.[34]

Finally, along the Rhine frontier the various tribes, especially the Burgundians and the Franks, were expanding into Roman territory, and the presence of a Gothic army to support the imperial forces could, in theory, give Constantius the manpower to combat the rolling slow annexation of imperial territory along the frontier.[35]

However, of foremost importance, the Goths were being transformed from 'enemies' into 'friends'. This allowed Constantius to withdraw troops that had been facing the Goths to fight in other theatres; for example Exuperantius in Armorica, or to form garrisons in newly-reconquered lands such as those in Hispania. As a result, Constantius was not compelled to either begin a new recruiting drive or to allocate funds to pay for troops to garrison areas facing the Goths. This saving in part negated the extra cost of allowing the Goths to settle in Aquitaine. Throughout the life of the Empire the great majority of the taxes collected were used to pay for the army. In theory, the Goths may now have been perceived as part of the army and, as such, the majority were now self-sufficient troops who did not need to be equipped by the state, and although they most likely would need paying for service, this would be only for their time in service, not on a permanent basis. The loss of revenue needed to pay the army was in effect being used to pay the 'army'.

On a more conjectural note, it is possible that Honorius – or more importantly Constantius – was aware that the land on both sides of the Pyrenees was home to members of the Theodosian dynasty, any of whom could declare themselves *Augustus* in opposition to Honorius, or, more likely, could be raised to the purple by others:[36] many of the aristocrats in southern Gaul still resented the earlier execution of the usurper Jovinus who had been one of their number, and Constantius may have been wary of these aristocrats pressuring a lesser member of the ruling dynasty to accept a nomination as emperor.[37] In addition, the near-run addition to the imperial family of Theodosius, son of Athaulf and Galla Placidia, may have caused paranoia in the heart of Constantius, a paranoia that would be focused on the region of Barcelona where Theodosius was buried.

As a final note, analysis has revealed that between the accession of Theodosius in the East and the compilation of the *Notitia Dignitatum* (dating to c.420) in the West, about half of the Western 'field army' had been lost.[38] In this context it was obviously necessary for Constantius to end the wars against the Goths, as otherwise the army could easily enter a process of rapid collapse. Furthermore, by bringing the Goths within the structure of the army, he would help to alleviate the problems of manpower shortage and, hopefully, be given time in which to recruit and rebuild.

Other Options

Yet there is one further question that remains with regard to the location of the Gothic establishment: that of where else they could have been settled. The Romans needed to maintain their lines of communication between Italy, Arles and Hispania, so the Goths could not be settled in the south of Gaul.[39] Constantius could have organized for them to live in Hispania, but there would be a strong possibility of the Goths declaring their independence, and the distance between Italy and Hispania was not conducive to lengthy military campaigns, as the absence of the army campaigning in Hispania would encourage attacks from across the northern borders.

For obvious reasons Italy was out of the question, and as the Goths would refuse to return across Italy to Illyricum, the only other alternative was northern Gaul. However, this option was also a risky one. The presence of the Franks, the Burgundians and the Alamanni meant that the Goths would be being settled in a region where loyalties were unpredictable. If the Goths reacted strongly against one of the other tribes, there would be a war along the Rhine which the Romans would struggle to control. Even more dangerous was the possibility that the Goths would ally with one or more of the tribes against Rome. With his limited resources, Constantius would be unable to face a combined barbarian assault. In effect, it is clear that Constantius arranged for the Goths to settle in the only region that was suitable both for the Goths and for Rome.

Given earlier examples of barbarian settlement, it also seems certain that the Roman government did not expect the Goths to remain independent for long. The fact that the Roman administrative system continued to function normally in Aquitania implies that the Goths were perceived as a 'friendly and obedient force' on Roman territory.[40] However, at least in part this was due to the fact that the Germanic peoples entering Roman territory had no political agenda of their own and no ideology that they wished to impose. As such, they found it 'most advantageous and profitable to work closely within the well-established and sophisticated structures of Roman life'.[41]

Of major importance to Constantius and Honorius, the settlement excluded the Goths from the Mediterranean, hence limiting the chance of yet another attempt by the Goths to reach Africa, a factor that may have caused friction between Rome and Toulouse later in the century.[42]

Gaul

For the majority of Gauls away from Aquitania, the treaty and settlement were a welcome relief. After more than a decade of war and usurpers, the settlement gave a respite to the war-weary provinces of Gaul and would hopefully give them the time they needed to recover, although the concept that the settlement allowed 'normal life to resume its course, though under new masters' may be a little too optimistic.[43] Following the treaty of 418/419 a degree of stability again appeared in the West, despite the tremendous losses previously suffered.[44] Further, the sparse written record demonstrates that in many cases the local 'Roman' aristocracy benefited from the change.

Despite the positive aspects of the settlement, there was one major negative aspect. The new Gothic regime chose Toulouse as a 'royal seat', a factor which differentiated it from earlier settlements. The use of the city as a 'capital' 'opened the way for the formation of a [Gothic Royal] court and a central administration where Roman and Gothic methods could combine'.[45] Despite the fact that the ruler in Toulouse had a 'dual personality, that of a Germanic king and that of a Roman patrician', in reality there was now a separate political entity inside the Roman Empire.

Hispania

The attacks by the Goths had seriously weakened the Siling Vandals and the Alans, to the point where they believed themselves to be too weak to continue as separate entities. As a result, they decided to leave their territories and place themselves under the command of Gunderic, the 'king' of the Asding Vandals in Gallaecia.[46] At an unknown point in time the king of the now combined Vandals and Alans took the title 'King of the Vandals and the Alans', a title later attested as being applied to Gelimer due to a silver *missorum* with the legend *Gailamir Rex Vandalorum et Alanorum*. As Gelimer ruled from 530 to 534, this illustrates that, despite their defeats, the Alans kept a separate identity within the Vandal kingdom.[47] Yet these are not the only peoples who joined forces under Gunderic. According to Possidius, 'There were Vandals and Alans, mixed with one of the Gothic peoples, and individuals of various nations.'[48] Without realizing it, the Roman plan to weaken the Vandals and Alans instead resulted in their coalescing to form a new Vandal 'super-group' that could rival that of the Goths themselves.[49] However, it would take time for the Vandal and Alan fugitives to be settled and integrated into the new enlarged kingdom.

Analysis

Alaric had demanded a military alliance, the rank of *magister militum*, a land grant close to the heart of the Empire, annual payments in gold, and large amounts of corn per year.[50] Although he had modified these terms in the face of Honorius' refusal to negotiate, they still suggest that he was hoping for many concessions from Honorius. His successor Athaulf had made similar demands, and had even married Galla Placidia and had a son with her. Of more interest, there is the statement that Athaulf wanted to support the Empire and believed that its fate was in his hands. Whether true or not, the fact that such a claim could be contemplated by Roman historians implies an arrogance on the part of the Goths not really in line with their true strength. The settlement in Gaul was, in reality, a compromise for both parties, with neither having a viable alternative option. In reality, the question in 418 was not one of how to come to an agreement, but of how the Romans would attempt to integrate an alien entity into the Empire and of how the Goths would resist.[51]

The Goths' long wanderings were finally over, but Wallia would not live to see them at peace: he died shortly after the move to Aquitania and he was succeeded by Theodoric.[52] Either before his elevation, or more likely shortly afterwards, in an attempt to cement his position Theodoric married Alaric's daughter.[53] The death of Wallia and accession of Theodoric probably caused consternation at the imperial court, but Theodoric was not in a position to demand changes: the settlement continued as planned, and Constantius was free to continue his attempt to further resolve affairs in the West.

Chapter Ten

The Recovery of the West

Constantius III and Honorius: 417

Despite the majority of both ancient and modern authors being focused on the Gothic settlement, there were other important events taking place between 417 and 419. Possibly the most important of these still involved Constantius. On 1 January 417, the *magister militum* Constantius entered into his second consulship, possibly as a reward for his efforts in defeating all the Gallic usurpers and for reducing the Goths to a position of subservience. Probably on the same day, he finally married Galla Placidia, the recently-released half-sister of Honorius, a marriage 'solemnized in the most dazzling fashion'.[1] It was not to be the happiest of marriages: Placidia's frequent rejections of Constantius had made him angry, especially at her attendants.[2] Nevertheless, they were to have two children: a daughter named Justa Grata Honoria – usually known simply as Honoria – was born in either late 417 or, more probably, in 418, and a son Valentinian, who was born on 2 July 419.[3]

Constantius' rise was now reaching its apogee. According to Olympiodorus, the change in Constantius' status from *magister militum* to member of the royal family caused a change in personality in Constantius: allegedly, he had been free from greed until he married Galla Placidia, after which he had a 'lust for money', a fact apparently confirmed by the fact that after his death 'Ravenna was inundated from all sides with law suits over his misappropriation of possessions.' Sadly for the dispossessed, the additional fact that Constantius had been married to Placidia, sister of the emperor, meant that they were to receive no compensation for their losses.[4]

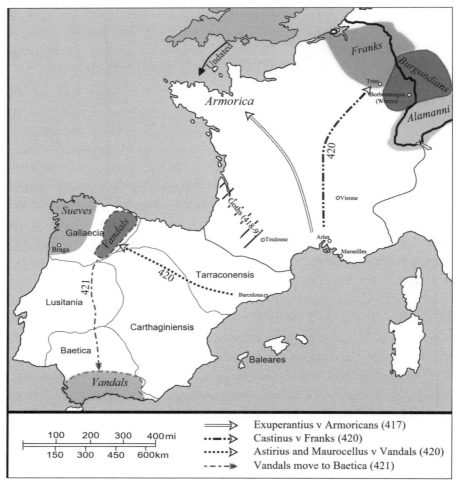

Map 12: Constantius' last Campaigns.

The Campaigns of 417

Apart from his marriage in January, Constantius was to be kept busy, both politically and militarily. On the political side, he was involved in the negotiations surrounding the Gothic settlement, both with the Goths and the Gallic nobles in Aquitania and the surrounding areas, but doubtless also with the court in Ravenna and the Senate in Rome.

Militarily, freed from the need to keep a large force in Hispania to blockade the Goths, Constantius took steps to reassert imperial dominance in the West, as despite the apparent resurgence of imperial power, affairs in the West remained in turmoil. The Roman government in Italy was in control of Italy and Africa, and insecurely held part of the Illyrian prefecture: in Hispania, Rome had 'retaken' Baetica and Lusitania, but the Sueves remained free and there was a new, extremely hostile conglomeration of Vandals and Alans in Gallaecia.[5]

It would appear that even before the death of Constantine III in 411, Britannia had renounced the usurper and attempted to realign with Honorius' court in Ravenna. Although Honorius would have welcomed the resurgence of patriotism in Britannia, affairs in Gaul and Hispania had prevented him from sending direct military aid. For the next generation life in Britannia would remain essentially 'Roman' in essence, but the citizens were forced to accept that they were no longer part of the Empire. Instead, they were reduced to appointing 'emperors' whose only rule was in Britannia. On the other hand, the evidence from writers such as Gildas implies that after only a short period this system became open to abuse, with 'emperors' rising and falling in swift succession.[6]

Although Roman in practice, the Britons had been forced to accept that they were on their own, at least as far as military matters were concerned (although trade appears to have continued). The Roman writers on the Continent were impressed by the resilience of the British and praised the fact that 'the British people took up arms, bore the brunt of the attack, and freed their cities from barbarian threat.'[7] Although it is usually accepted that the main attacks came from the Saxons across the North Sea and from the Picts in Scotland, perhaps the main threat for many of the British came from Ireland: by the early fifth century the Irish had begun to establish many settlements along the western coast of Britannia.[8]

On the mainland, and despite the positive mentions in the sources, only the southern part of Gaul was being ruled directly. In northern Gaul, the Alamanni had crossed the Upper Rhine, the Burgundians had settled around Borbetomagus (Worms), the Franks were expanding their control in the north-eastern regions along the Rhine, and the north-west was being disturbed by internal unrest and possibly immigrations from Britannia (see above). In these regions control was being left to Roman magnates, only occasionally being supported by help from Rome.[9] In addition, due to the recent usurpations and the barbarian inroads across the Rhine, the centre of Roman government in Gaul had moved from Trier, now 'critically exposed', on the Rhine frontier, to Arles, deep in the south.[10]

With his army freed from shadowing the Goths, Constantius was finally in a position to begin the reconquest of Gaul. In 417 he sent a military force under a commander named Exuperantius to restore Roman rule in Armorica.[11] In one campaign, Exuperantius defeated the 'rebels' and the whole of north-western Gaul was apparently finally back under imperial rule for the first time since the barbarian invasion across the Rhine in 406. Nevertheless, Armorica was to remain a region on the fringes of Roman rule, possibly from as early as 418 (see below) but definitely later, when the trickle of immigrants from Britannia became a flood.

418

If not before, following the treaty of 418 and the decimation of Vandals and Alans, Roman troops freed from shadowing the Goths – and probably including those who had defected from Gerontius to join Constantius in 411 – were finally able to return to Hispania in strength.[12] Some of these may have been sent to Baetica and Lusitania to begin the process of regaining complete control of the provinces following the retreat of the Silings and the Alans to Gallaecia.

With regard to Britannia, there is a (usually overlooked) notice in the Anglo-Saxon Chronicle (ASC): 'A.D. 418. This year the Romans collected all the hoards of gold that were in Britannia; and some they hid in the earth, so that no man afterwards might find them, and some they carried away with them into Gaul.'

Although the ASC is not regarded as trustworthy for its entries at this early date due to the distance in time between these events and the composition of the text, the passage does record a tradition that at some point in the early fifth century the 'Romans' uprooted from Britannia and crossed to Gaul. This event is most likely to be associated with the known emigration of large numbers of Britons, who settled in Armorica, an area later known as Brittany ('Little Britannia', as opposed to the 'Great (Larger) Britain' they left behind). It is quite likely that at least some of the disturbances recorded in Armorica at this time were caused by the influx of immigrants from Britannia: it is possible that this included many who were disenchanted with Roman rule due to the reluctance of the Empire to send troops to defend the island, and so promoted 'insurrection', or at least passive resistance.[13]

The Council of the Seven Gauls

In 418 there was also a major political event, whose importance to our understanding of the situation in Gaul is easily overlooked. The Council of the Seven Provinces (*Concilium septem provinciarum*, sometimes 'Council of the Seven Gauls') had been established during the earlier supremacy of Stilicho, probably in 402. Following the usurpations of Constantine III and Jovinus the council had lapsed, but it was re-established by order of Honorius on 17 April 418 in the *Constitutio saluberrima* (more properly, the *Saluberrima magnificentiae*).[14] At approximately the same time Honorius and Constantius adopted a policy of preferring native Gauls in Gallic offices (see below).[15]

The council met between 13 August and 13 September, although two of the provinces in which the Goths were being settled were allowed to send deputies rather than senior officials, likely due to the latter being intimately involved in the process of settling the Goths.[16] It has been suggested that the revival of the council suggests that Rome was determined to organize a 'retrenchment' in the south of Gaul.[17]

In this context, it is important to note that the removal of the headquarters of the prefecture of the Gallic provinces from Trier to Arles implies that Honorius and Constantius were effectively acknowledging that they had either lost or had incomplete control of the ten provinces of northern Gaul.[18] In addition, the 'Seven Gauls' was roughly an area enclosed by the River Loire and it would appear that in 418 it was only this area that was under effective Roman rule.[19] In effect, the Goths were being settled on the 'western flank' of a 'new' Roman frontier.[20]

Of equal importance, the letter detailing the creation of the council makes it clear that Honorius and Constantius still saw the region being settled by the Goths as remaining an integral part of the Roman Empire.[21] There was as yet no concept of there being an independent Gothic kingdom within the Empire.

As just noted, in addition to the council, Constantius made an attempt to lure the local aristocracy back to supporting Ravenna. Prior to 406 the office of Gallic prefect had been occupied by officials sent from Italy. Doubtless this had contributed to the feeling of alienation of the Gallic aristocracy which had resulted in their readiness to support Constantine III and the later usurpation of Jovinus. After 418 the post of Gallic prefect was almost always given to members of the Gallic aristocracy; a means of ensuring the Gauls' adherence to Rome.

Yet there are two ways in which both the formation of the council and the decision to appoint Gauls to important offices failed to complete the reorientation of Gaul. One is the fact that as only southern regions were represented at the council, the implication is that a large part of central and northern Gaul was 'at best intermittently governed'.[22] The second is that, despite the attempts at conciliation, the usurpations in Gaul and Britannia had demonstrated that many in the Gallic aristocracy were unhappy with the rule of Ravenna, and for those Gauls who were completely alienated from the court in Ravenna, or who had supported the usurpers and so were concerned about their future, the Gothic court in Toulouse would eventually give them readier access to influence and power.[23]

Analysis

As a consequence of these deliberations and despite the fact that the settlement should probably still be seen as detrimental to the affairs of the Empire in the long term, at the time the benefits may have been seen as outweighing the shortcomings. In fact, the adoption of the policy of creating allies out of the invaders may have been the main reason why the West survived the invasions and civil wars of the early fifth century.[24] It is largely with the benefit of hindsight and the knowledge of what ramifications the policy would have in the long term that the negative aspects of Constantius' decision can be seen as outweighing the positives.

With the Goths settling in Aquitania, at least part of Gaul recovered, Baetica and Lusitania once more completely under Roman occupation and Africa reintegrated into the Empire, Constantius had effectively restored the fortunes of the Empire. The only 'permanent loss' at this point was Britannia, and although the loss of the British grain supply was a blow, the fact that Britannia no longer needed an imperially-financed army and was in no position to raise yet another usurper helped to offset the political damage. Constantius' control at the head of the army was now far more secure than that of Stilicho.

As if to reinforce his secure position, on 2 July 418 Placidia gave birth to a son, Valentinian.[25] Since Honorius was childless and seemed destined to remain so, the baby Valentinian was nominally the next in line to the throne. As father to the heir, Constantius' position seemed even more secure than before.

Theodoric, King of the Visigoths

Despite the positivity surrounding Constantius, there was one major event in 418 that was to have a major impact upon the future: even as the Goths were being settled in Aquitania, Wallia died. Although it has been claimed that Wallia was an 'obedient tool' for Constantius, in reality he had had little option but to accept the settlement organized by Constantius.[26] His successor was Theodoric.[27] Theodoric was almost certainly a better politician than Alaric, Athaulf and Wallia.[28] However, he had one major advantage over his predecessors: he ruled a semi-autonomous people settled in Gaul for thirty-three years, giving him ample time to learn his craft and use his experience to the advantage of the Goths, who, after their final settlement in Aquitania, are usually known as 'Visigoths' ('Western Goths'), to differentiate them from their cousins who were simultaneously making a name for themselves in the East.

The nature of the settlement, as noted above, is open to interpretation. However, there are notices, especially in the later Visigothic law codes, that have implications for many aspects of the Visigoths' relations to Romans in their territories. The main factor is that there was a law forbidding the intermarriage of Goths and Romans.[29] Although working from later evidence, it is possible to propose that, even from the first settlement, and possibly initiated by Theodoric, the Visigoths were aware of the Roman record of amalgamating settlers into their own polity and were determined to remain a separate politic entity.[30]

419

Although there had been an apparent resurgence of Roman power, problems continued to arise. By 419 it is likely that Roman troops were once more securing the majority of Hispania, but at the same time a quarrel broke out between Gunderic, king of the Vandals, and Hermeric, king of the Sueves, in Gallaecia. The cause of the argument is unknown, but probably concerned the presence in Gallaecia of the usurper Maximus, as will be hypothesized below. Whatever the cause, the Vandals attacked and managed to lay siege to the Suevic army in the 'Erbasian Mountains', the precise location of which is unknown.[31]

In addition, probably in 419, but perhaps later in 420, the Franks attacked and sacked Trier. Although the Gothic problem was apparently solved, the West was still facing considerable pressure along the frontiers and in Hispania.

420

Notwithstanding the ongoing difficulties, in January 420 Constantius was appointed consul for the third time.[32] In addition, and in imitation of Stilicho, Constantius also received the title *parens principum* ('first parent' or 'parental guardian') in 420.[33]

Determined to continue the recovery, when the campaign season of 420 opened Constantius definitely initiated a first and possibly ordered a second campaign aimed at further recovering lost ground. Usually dated to either 419 or 420 but most likely the latter, one of these was the dispatch of the *magister* Castinus to northern Gaul in a campaign against the Franks, almost certainly in response to the sacking of Trier.[34] There is no other mention of this campaign, but as the sources are mainly focused upon events in Hispania, this is not unexpected. In spite of the lack of other evidence, the apparent peace along the Rhine frontier for the next two years suggests that the campaign was a success, with the Franks being pushed back from the city and remaining peaceful as long as Constantius was alive.

The second campaign definitely occurred. In Hispania, the *vicarius* Maurocellus and the *Comes Hispaniae* Astirius advanced into Gallaecia in 'command of a very great army and the outcome of a very great war'.[35] This was ostensibly aimed at relieving the siege of the Sueves by the Vandals in the Erbasian Mountains.[36]

What actually happened in this campaign is unclear, as the report given by Hydatius requires detailed analysis in order to reach a conclusion. Strangely, despite the related capture of Maximus during the campaign, Hydatius makes no mention of him, simply stating that 'After a dispute had arisen between Gunderic, king of the Vandals, and Hermeric, king of the Sueves, the Sueves were besieged in the Erbasian Mountains by the Vandals.'[37] It is possible that Gunderic was attempting to force the Sueves to join with his forces, so making him undisputedly the strongest military leader in Hispania.[38] Sadly, the precise location of the 'Erbasian Mountains' is unknown, as a result of which it is uncertain whether the Vandals invaded Suevian territory or vice versa.

A close assessment of Hydatius makes it possible that, contrary to popular opinion, the Sueves had demanded that the Vandals, including the survivors of the Gothic attacks, join them.[39] The reason for the confusion can be found in a second relevant passage in Hydatius, which as usual is open to interpretation:

> The Vandals were dissuaded from their siege of the Sueves by pressure from Astirius, the *Comes Hispaniarum*, and after some men under the command of the *vicarius* Maurocellus were killed in their flight from Braga, the rest of [the Vandals] left Gallaecia behind and crossed into Baetica.
>
> *Hydatius 66 [74] s.a. 420.*[40]

The first thing of note here is that, despite some modern assumptions, nowhere is Astirius given credit for defeating the Vandals in a set-piece battle: instead, it is the threat of attack from both the Romans outside and the Sueves inside the siege lines that forced the Vandals to raise the siege.

Furthermore, the *vicarius* Maurocellus was not present at the siege. Instead, 'some men under the command of the *vicarius* Maurocellus were killed in their flight from Braga.' Rather than being with Astirius, Maurocellus had been sent to Braga, the 'capital' of the Suevic territory, and had fled from there in some haste, being attacked and losing some men in the process. Why a Roman force would be present at the Suevic capital is nowhere explained.

Even more perplexing is that although Maurocellus was defeated and forced to flee from Braga, and although Astirius had not actually defeated the Vandals, Astirius was unaccountably honoured with the title of *patricius* shortly after the campaign.[41] Consequently, the whole episode is usually interpreted by modern historians as a major victory for the Romans, with dissenting historians being few.[42] This is confusing, unless Astirius had actually accomplished his mission.

Analysis

The only narrative that fits all the known information, as well as explaining later events, is that the main force under Astirius was advancing towards the Erbasian Mountains, but that the main objective was not the Vandals, but the usurper Maximus: barbarians were almost always less important than usurpers in the priorities of the Roman government.[43]

Assigned the task of capturing Maximus, only as he approached the mountains did Astirius learn that Maximus was being supported by the Sueves, and that, rather than being involved in the siege, Maximus had remained in Braga. Aware that the majority of the Suevic army was trapped by the Vandals, Astirius sent a small detachment under Maurocellus to attempt the capture of Maximus. In the meantime, Astirius advanced a little nearer to the mountains, pinning both the Vandals and the Sueves, so giving Maurocellus time to fulfil his mission.

Threatened by the Romans in their rear, the Vandals had little option but to raise the siege. Yet there needs to be an explanation for Astirius' failure to use his military supremacy to inflict a major defeat on either the Sueves or the Vandals. This is because his orders were the elimination of Maximus, not a risky military engagement.

Instead, Maurocellus managed to infiltrate Braga and capture Maximus, being attacked by Sueves from the city as he escaped but still managing to evade capture with the loss of only a few men. The elimination of Maximus with so few losses is the main reason why Astirius was rewarded with the title of *patricius*. Maximus himself was sent to Honorius, probably in late 420 or early 421, and was later to be paraded in 422 at Honorius' thirtieth anniversary.[44]

As a consequence of these events, either late in 420 or possibly more likely in 421, the Vandals relocated to the more hospitable region of Baetica, possibly moving to the regions previously held by the Silings.[45] Yet it should be noted that many years after the move the Vandals are recorded by Hydatius as attacking Hispalis (Seville), the main city in the province. Consequently, the modern assumption that they immediately took control of the whole province is mistaken. Nevertheless, the new Vandal army was at war with Rome and remained a major threat to the security of Hispania.

421: Emperor Constantius III

Although the Vandals were emerging as a major destabilizing force in Hispania, slowly the Western Empire was becoming more secure. Yet although Constantius was having success in re-establishing the West, the evidence suggests that, however grateful he was for Constantius' work on behalf of the Empire, Honorius was unwilling to accede to growing demands for Constantius to be promoted to co-*Augustus* and was extremely unhappy when he was finally forced to allow this to happen.[46] Where these demands were coming from is unrecorded, but it is likely that the main pressure was coming from Placidia and her supporters. In the future, Placidia would continuously press for her son Valentinian to be accepted as the legitimate heir to the Western throne, so it is highly likely that it was under her guidance that pressure was brought on Honorius to promote Constantius, a move that would simultaneously secure Valentinian as the future heir. Olympiodorus writes that the acclamation of Constantius was 'out of respect for his familial relationship' following the birth of Valentinian, perhaps supporting the hypothesis that Placidia was the moving force behind the acclamation.[47]

Consequently, on 8 February 421 Constantius was appointed co-emperor with Honorius.[48] Honorius and Constantius then jointly acclaimed Placidia as *Augusta* and Valentinian was declared *nobilissimus* (most noble).[49]

Although no doubt an honour, Constantius soon regretted the elevation, since after he became emperor his movements were heavily circumscribed and he no longer had the freedom he had enjoyed as *magister militum*.[50] It is possible that this assertion was to affect the generals who came after him, since the vast majority of them had no wish to place themselves upon the throne, possibly due to the knowledge that once emperor, they would be heavily tied down by bureaucratic red tape and so unable to lead the army in person, thereby being at risk of losing the army's support.

Alongside his regret, at this point things began to go further awry for Constantius: despite his obvious service to the West, when notice of his elevation was sent to Theodosius II in the East, the Eastern emperor refused to acknowledge Constantius as *Augustus*, Placidia as *Augusta* or Valentinian as *nobilissimus*.[51] In response, Constantius allegedly immediately began to prepare for war with the East.[52]

Although the truth of this claim is sometimes questioned, the Eastern court was obviously expecting some form of military action in the Balkans: Theodosius quickly attempted to settle affairs on the eastern frontier with Persia in preparation for a war in the Balkans, but unfortunately his plans were thrown into confusion when his attempted settlement instead provoked a war with Persia.

In truth, Theodosius had given Constantius a pretext for a project which Constantius' predecessor Stilicho had first planned: the forcible annexation of the Illyrian recruiting grounds. During the war with the Goths after their victory over the Eastern Roman army at the Battle of Adrianople in 378, the Western emperor Gratian had allocated control of the prefecture of Illyricum – obviously including the main recruiting region for the Western army – to the new Eastern emperor Theodosius I. This was because the Goths were ravaging the region between Constantinople and the Julian Alps, so were crossing and re-crossing the boundary between the Eastern and Western Empires. By allocating Illyricum, Gratian ensured that there would be no division of command during the ensuing Gothic War. After the war had been concluded in 382 and due to rising tensions between East and West, Illyricum had not been returned to the West. Consequently, the West had lost the source of its best recruits and both Stilicho and now Constantius would look for pretexts upon which to re-establish their control of the region.

As Constantius began the preparations for war, he began to feel ill. These were the early symptoms of pleurisy, an excessive collection of fluid in the pleural cavity.[53] The pleura are two large, thin layers of tissue that separate the lungs from the chest wall. One pleural layer of tissue wraps around the outside of the lungs, and the other lines the inner chest wall. Between these two layers is a small space that is usually filled with a very small amount of liquid. Normally, these layers act like two pieces of smooth satin gliding past each other, allowing the lungs to expand and contract with each breath. With pleurisy, these tissues swell and become inflamed. As a result, the two layers of the pleural membrane rub against each other like two pieces of sandpaper.[54] Consequently, Constantius' symptoms would have included chest pain, shortness of breath and possibly a cough or a fever. It is possible that he had the symptoms prior to his elevation to the throne, but this is unlikely: the average life expectancy for malignant pleurisy is a little less than six months, with survival sometimes being less than four months.

Due to his illness, and before he could begin any new campaign against the East, Constantius died on 2 September 421.[55] It is probable that it was the speed of his deterioration and death that caused Theophanes and Michael the Syrian to claim that he was murdered, although these are the only two sources that make such a claim.[56]

The earlier death of Wallia and accession of Theodoric had probably caused consternation at the imperial court. The death of Constantius in 421 was to cause further difficulties. In many cases, treaties in late antiquity were assumed to be between individuals. That between Wallia and Constantius had been 'negated' by the former's death in 418, but Theodoric had not been in a position to demand changes. Now, with the death of Constantius, Theodoric may have felt that he had a 'free hand' in Gaul, although he would need to be careful, as the Empire was still a force to be reckoned with. Theodoric would only attempt to attack the Empire when it was distracted by events elsewhere, which would happen with regrettable repetition during the remainder of Theodoric's long reign. Of far more importance, Theodoric was in a position to assert his independence from Ravenna, meaning that the Visigoths would not now become integrated into the Empire.[57] Large parts of Gaul would now become permanently lost to the Empire.

Chapter Eleven

Aftermath and Conclusions

After Constantius

T he death of Constantius appears to have created a new power battle between 'factions' at court. There were at least two of these, with one focusing upon the emperor and the other upon Placidia. In either 420 or 421, Honorius had appointed an individual by the name of Castinus to be the *Comes domesticorum* (Count of the Household).[1] In this position Castinus had led a campaign against the Franks (see above, Chapter 10).[2] Probably at the beginning of 422, after the death of Constantius III, Honorius elevated Castinus to *dux*, before shortly afterwards making him *magister utriusque militiae* (Master of all the Troops). Castinus was to lead the faction supporting Honorius.

In 422 Castinus was ordered to lead a campaign against the Vandals in Hispania, being given a mixed force of Romans and Gothic troops from the new settlement in Aquitania.[3] In an unexpected turn of events, another Roman general was ordered to accompany him. Boniface had risen to fame as early as 413, when the Goths under Athaulf had attacked Marseilles during the conflict between Athaulf and Constantius III (see above, Chapter 7). During the attack Boniface had managed to wound Athaulf himself, a feat for which he was 'fêted by the citizens'.[4] Following this moment of fame, Boniface successfully commanded troops in Africa in 417 and entered into correspondence with (St) Augustine, in the course of which Augustine allayed Boniface's Christian fears that fighting wars and killing was against God's will and would ensure 'eternal damnation'.[5] Boniface was to lead the faction supporting Placidia.

His recall may have been an attempt by Placidia to bring in an opponent capable of preventing Castinus from achieving the exalted status of Constantius. However, the two commanders quarrelled and Castinus attempted to have Boniface dismissed, as a result of which Boniface fled back to Africa where he had established a personal power base.[6] Castinus appeared to have firmly established himself as the leading power at court.

Despite the loss of Boniface and his troops, in 422 Castinus invaded Baetica in a campaign against the Vandals. The Vandals were outmanoeuvred and placed under siege. At this point, Castinus made a grave mistake and offered battle. He was defeated, allegedly thanks to the treachery of the Gothic troops enlisted to fight alongside the Romans. Although no reason for this 'treachery' is given, it is possible that Castinus had attempted to use the Goths in a similar manner to that of Theodosius I at the Battle of the Frigidus in 394. Then Theodosius had sent the Goths to attack in the first wave and they had been decimated, with the result that Alaric had revolted and set out upon the long route to the Sack of Rome. It is possible that Castinus attempted the same tactic, with the same result. On the other hand, it may simply have been a catastrophic defeat in battle, for which the blame was laid at the feet of the Goths rather than any Roman being at fault. Defeated, Castinus was forced to retire to Tarraco, while the Vandals were left secure in Baetica.[7]

Possibly as a reaction to her political defeat and the retreat of Boniface, Placidia appears to have changed tack, attempting to secure her influence by becoming close to her brother; according to the sources, rather too close.[8]

Castinus, Boniface and Aetius

Placidia was a very forceful woman. Brought up in the household of Stilicho and Serena, in all likelihood she still aimed at emulating their political and military domination of Honorius, although without the title of *parens principum*. She was now in opposition to Castinus, who as the *magister militum* clearly saw himself as the natural heir to Stilicho and Constantius III.[9] The scene was set for a bitter rivalry. Although the advantage may have been with Castinus, since he controlled the army, Placidia was known to be ruthless: in 408, when Rome was being besieged by the Goths under Alaric, she had allegedly approved the Senate's decision to kill Serena, the adopted half-sister who had raised her. Sentiment was not a strong part of Placidia's personality.

Rather than taking the blame for his defeat in Hispania, Castinus claimed that his failure was the result of a plot against him by Placidia,

Boniface and the Goths.[10] Whether his claim was true or not is unknown, but in the circumstances a conspiracy under the auspices of Placidia and Boniface remains a strong possibility. This is reinforced by the fact that when news of the defeat reached Ravenna, Honorius and Placidia quarrelled. Shortly after, Placidia fled to Constantinople.[11] Boniface, however, secure in Africa, remained loyal to Placidia rather than Honorius, and even helped her by sending her money.[12]

The Death of Honorius

All these political machinations were to count for little: in August 423 Honorius died, like his father Theodosius, of dropsy.[13] Despite the modern conviction that by this time the Empire was divided, in contemporary society it was still seen as a single entity, even allowing for the convention of having two separate rulers, so the West waited for Theodosius II, emperor of the East, to make a decision regarding who should rule the West.

At first Castinus appears to have wanted Theodosius to accept the role of sole emperor. This would have been an ideal situation, since in this event Castinus would become the effective ruler of the West. However, in Constantinople Placidia was haranguing Theodosius into accepting the rights of her son Valentinian – who was now 4 years old – to become the next emperor in Italy. Doubtless Castinus heard of Placidia's attempts to promote Valentinian in Constantinople. If Valentinian was installed as emperor, Placidia would become the effective ruler in the West, in which case Castinus' days were numbered.

There would have been many who supported Placidia in her attempt to restore the 'House of Theodosius'. Into this group fell Boniface, largely due to his apparent personal connections to Placidia. No doubt he, and others, also felt that they would profit from Placidia's gratitude when her son was set upon the throne. In fact, Boniface was to benefit from his support of Placidia almost instantly. Before deciding upon the identity of the new emperor, and possibly as a reward for his loyalty to Placidia, it would appear that Theodosius appointed Boniface *Comes Africae* (Count of Africa). It was now certain that Boniface would maintain his support for the Theodosian dynasty.

John

Yet for unknown reasons, Theodosius II failed to make a quick decision. As a consequence, Castinus decided to take a fateful step. Emulating Western *magistri* of the past, he decided to act on his own initiative. On 20 November 423 he appointed John, the *Primicerius Notariorum* (Head of the Secretaries), as the new emperor of the West.[14] Placidia's supporters no doubt fled from Rome and took refuge either in the East or on their own estates. Their places would be taken by loyal supporters of Castinus and John.

John was crowned in Rome, before travelling to Ravenna.[15] His first act was to send an embassy to Constantinople in an attempt to gain recognition for his elevation. At the same time, the embassy was to propose Castinus as the West's nominee for consul in 424. The embassy failed.[16] Furthermore, the ambassadors were badly treated and exiled around the East.[17] It was clear that Theodosius was intent on removing John from power.

Exuperantius and Aetius

Before the reply from Constantinople arrived, it is clear that John made several appointments to the senior positions of command in the West. Included in these was Aetius, who had spent several years as a hostage of the Huns. In addition, a man named Gaudentius was appointed *magister equitum*, Castinus remaining in the senior post of *magister peditum*. The only other appointment of which we can be certain is that of an individual named Exuperantius, almost certainly the same who had earlier campaigned in Gaul, who came from Poitiers in the centre of Gaul and was appointed as *Praefectus Praetorio per Galliarum* (Praetorian Prefect of Gaul).[18] The promotion of a Gaul to the post may have been intended by John as an attempt to ensure Gallic loyalty.

Unfortunately for John, alongside these developments the continued animosity between Castinus and Boniface had immediate repercussions. Unsurprisingly, in Africa Boniface refused to accept John's claim to be emperor. Boniface immediately cut the supplies of grain from Africa to Italy.[19] This was bad news, especially for the citizens of Rome. There was now no doubt that there would be a civil war.

It would appear that John ordered a campaign, dispatching a picked force – including Huns – from Italy to recapture Africa.[20] However, the main effect of the campaign being sent to Africa was to leave John too weak to consider any further pre-emptive manoeuvres in Italy.[21] Instead, he was forced to remain on the defensive as soon as the expedition left.

In Gaul, John's attempt to curry favour by the appointment of Exuperantius failed. Although many would have been opposed to John's position as an usurper, his decision to submit clerics to secular jurisdiction also caused offence and may imply that he had 'Arian tendencies'.[22]

To add to the confusion, the army in Gaul decided to mutiny and the troops in Arles killed Exuperantius.[23] Moreover, the Gallic Chronicler in the entry for 425 states that 'Count Gaudentius…was killed by the soldiers in Gaul.'[24] No doubt the troops involved hoped that by killing Gaudentius they would gain favour with the soon-to-be-restored Theodosian imperial court. Unfortunately for John, he had no troops to spare to avenge either Exuperantius or Gaudentius, and he was forced to remain inactive.[25] It was now certain that there would be no help from the West for the army of Italy.

In addition, the Visigoths under King Theoderic refused to support the new regime. Instead of supplying troops for Castinus again, Theoderic appears to have seen the impending civil war as an opportunity to enlarge his dominions in Gaul. Furthermore, at unknown dates in the 420s the Franks may have attacked and captured Cambrai and Tournai, and the period during which John usurped the throne and the West was in chaos would appear to be the most likely time for their incursions.[26]

Boniface, Valentinian and Aetius

At some point in 424 the West's expedition to Africa set sail. Far from regaining Africa and giving John a military victory, the campaign ended in defeat and one of the major outcomes was to ensure that the forces that John had at his disposal to face the upcoming war against Theodosius II were less effective.[27] The other was to weaken military and political support for John's reign.

Furthermore, Theodosius now confirmed his backing for Placidia and Valentinian. They were sent to Thessalonica and, reversing his decision in 421 to not accept Valentinian as *nobilissimus* and Placidia as *Augusta*,

Theodosius officially invested Valentinian as *Caesar* on 23 October 424.[28] As a further sign of the new-found concord between Theodosius and Placidia, Theodosius belatedly recognized the appointment of Constantius III as emperor of the West in 421, three years after the event, thus ensuring Valentinian's recognition as the son and heir of the deceased emperor.[29] To command the expedition against John, Theodosius appointed Ardabur, the Eastern *magister utriusque militiae*, along with Ardabur's son Aspar.[30] With them was Candidianus, possibly a fellow *magister militum* to Ardabur.[31]

In late 424, and in desperation, John turned to Aetius. Recognizing the need for large numbers of reliable troops, John ordered Aetius to go to the Huns with a large sum of gold in the hope that Aetius could obtain their support.[32] Aetius had faith in his relationships with the new Hunnic kings Rua and Octar, having grown up alongside them for many years. Aetius accepted the mission and began the long journey back to the Hunnic lands.[33]

The Campaign in the West

At the beginning of the campaign season of 425 the Eastern commander Ardabur decided to divide his forces, Ardabur himself leading the naval forces, while Aspar and Candidianus led the rest of the army by the land route into Italy. By means of a fast advance, Aspar managed to surprise John, and before a warning could be sounded he captured the city of Aquileia. Placidia and Valentinian joined him in the city.[34]

For Ardabur, events took a completely different path. While at sea he was blown off course and his vessel, together with two other triremes, was captured by forces loyal to John, although mistakenly he was to be well-treated.[35] Ardabur took advantage of the situation. Allowed to wander at will due to John's decision to treat him kindly, he began talking to John's senior officers. These men had probably already begun to regret their support for John. After all, his campaign in Africa had failed and now news arrived that Aspar had already taken Aquileia.[36] Yet there may be one further reason for their change of allegiance. Olympiodorus claims that Ardabur 'suborned the generals that had been retired from their commands'.[37] It would appear that, alongside the promotion of Exuperantius and Aetius, John had promoted trusted men to senior posts within the army. The men who had been replaced remained with the army but, obviously, their loyalty to John had been damaged. Although an alternative translation, this explains the willingness of these officers to come to an agreement with Ardabur.

Ardabur now sent a message to his son Aspar, telling him to travel 'as though to a victory assured'.[38] Aspar followed his father's orders, travelling quickly to Ravenna and being guided across the marshes surrounding the city.[39] Finding the gates open, Aspar took control of Ravenna, doubtless helped by the army under John which at this point almost certainly decided to change their allegiance.

John himself was captured in Ravenna and was sent under guard to Placidia and Valentinian, who had remained in Aquileia when Aspar attacked Ravenna. Once in Aquileia John was taken to the hippodrome, where he was mutilated by having his hand cut off and was then paraded on a donkey, before finally being executed by decapitation.[40]

Aetius

Three days after the execution of John, Aetius returned to Italy leading a large force of Huns.[41] Unaware of John's death, Aetius immediately attacked the Eastern army. After heavy losses on both sides a truce was agreed, probably after messages reached Aetius that John and Gaudentius were dead.[42] Aetius was enough of a realist to acknowledge that his position as a rebel was hopeless. In the circumstances, he did the only thing that he could: he used the threat of the Huns as a bargaining point to negotiate with Placidia, now acting as regent for her son.

Aetius accepted the position of a high-ranking military officer in the new regime.[43] In return, he negotiated a treaty with the Huns. They were paid a large amount of gold as compensation for their travel and losses, and after an exchange of hostages and oaths the Huns departed for home.[44] However, Placidia would never forget that Aetius had supported John against her son: the two would remain political opponents and she would not hesitate to manipulate him in her attempts to 'foil the ambitions of any general who showed signs of becoming too powerful for her liking'.[45]

Having secured the West, Placidia and Valentinian travelled to Rome where, on 23 October 425, Valentinian was proclaimed emperor by Helion, cousin of Theodosius II. Valentinian was just 6 years old. Upon securing the throne, Placidia made a man named Felix the new *magister militum praesentalis*, at the same time giving him the title *patricius*.[46] Nothing is known about Felix before this appointment.

One of the first decisions of the new regime was to send Castinus into exile rather than have him executed.[47] Castinus' decision to maintain a low profile during John's reign saved him from death.[48] In the hope of gaining support, and in recognition that Rome had still not fully recovered from the sack by the Goths, in early 426 one of the main taxes on the city of Rome and the Senate, the *aurum oblaticium*, was remitted by the new emperor.[49] The latest civil war was over and the House of Theodosius was again established on the Western throne.

Conclusions

As noted in the Introduction, Constantius' reputation as both military commander and emperor has suffered in the centuries since his death. In some respects, this may be due to the fact that his long supremacy (c.410–421) and his actions in restoring the strength of the West have been eclipsed by the fact that he settled the Goths in Gaul and that he ruled as emperor for only a few months in 421. In addition, the claim that as emperor he planned to campaign against the East has resulted in the perception of his abilities being tarnished from a very early date.

It was not always like this: in Constantius' own time he was given the title *reparator rei publicanae* (Restorer of the Republic), but as early as the compilation of the *Gallic Chronicle of 452* – less than forty years after his death – he had already been 'reduced to a minor figure', a harbinger of the lack of interest in his reign that was to last for more than 1,500 years.[50]

The main cause of his 'disappearance' must be that his supremacy is between those of Stilicho and Aetius. The lives of both these men have been regularly reassessed.[51] The majority view is that Stilicho was the 'strong arm' of Honorius up to 406, defeating Radagaisus and controlling Alaric. It was only his desire to go to war with the East and the subsequent invasion of Gaul by 'massed barbarians' that are used to demonstrate that he had lost control at this late date in his supremacy.

In this view, the subsequent Sack of Rome clearly demonstrates the ability of Stilicho and the lack of ability of his successors, at least until the rise of Aetius. Between 408 and 423 the actions of Honorius and his military commanders are continuously downplayed, with Honorius especially being vilified (see above, Chapter 5):

> At that time they say that the Emperor Honorius in Ravenna received the message from one of the eunuchs, evidently a keeper of the poultry, that Rome had perished. And he cried out and said, 'And yet it has just eaten from my hands!' For he had a very large cockerel, Rome by name; and the eunuch comprehending his words said that it was the city of Rome which had perished at the hands of Alaric, and the emperor with a sigh of relief answered quickly: 'But I thought that my fowl Rome had perished.' So great, they say, was the folly with which this emperor was possessed.
>
> *Procopius, The Vandal War, 3.2.25–26.*

The attitude portrayed by Procopius has been transferred by intervening historians to his court, with little effort being made to stop the Goths from promenading through Italy at will. The analysis of events detailed above, and especially those concerning Honorius' attempts to defend Rome, demonstrate that this perception is false, and that the main difficulty facing Honorius and his generals was that the strength of Alaric's forces meant that risking a battle was fraught with danger, as a single defeat could doom Honorius to deposition and death. It was only when Constantius, a man confident in his military abilities, took control that a definite policy was adopted and the recovery was begun.

After the deaths of Constantius and Honorius the rearguard fought by Aetius in his attempts to maintain the integrity of the West are often highlighted as examples of how the West could have survived had he only lived longer. These assessments almost always neglect to include the full impact of his failures, the most obvious of which are the loss of Africa and its revenues to the Vandals and the increasing independence of the Goths in Gaul. His reputation was secured with the defeat of Attila the Hun at the Battle of the Catalaunian Plains in 451: Constantius had no equivalent victory with which to secure his own reputation.

The reputations of Stilicho and Aetius were augmented by praise in the surviving panegyrics of Claudian (Stilicho) and Merobaudes (Aetius). There is no equivalent work for Constantius. On the contrary, his accomplishments are acknowledged but then weighed against the negatives of his supremacy, especially his decision to settle the Goths in Gaul. Consequently, his 'reign' is usually seen as mainly negative, with the loss of part of southern Gaul to the Goths and the subsequent growth of the Gothic kingdom being his main 'failure'. Alongside this is the activity in Hispania that resulted in the formation of a stronger barbarian group under Gunderic and then Gaiseric being both in a position to dominate much of Hispania and, subsequently, cross to Africa and conquer the richest province of the Western Empire.

Although these criticisms are undoubtedly accurate to some degree, they rely upon a hindsight that was – obviously – not available to Constantius. When seen in context, the majority of Constantius' actions and decisions are prudent and aimed at solving the problems he faced at that specific time. The main criticism he faces is the settlement of the Goths, but the above analysis clearly demonstrates that, in this, he had little alternative but to settle the Goths within the Empire, and that the settlement in Gaul was the only available option. Hence, it is here postulated that the criticism of this decision is at fault and is only viable when seen in hindsight.

A more sustainable condemnation concerns events in Hispania. There is no indication that there were any conflicts between Rome/Ravenna and the Siling Vandals, the Asding Vandals, the Alans or the Sueves in the years between the death of Gerontius and the arrival of the Goths in Barcelona. The decision of Constantius/Honorius to unleash the Goths upon the Alans and Siling Vandals following the treaty of 416 may have been justified to some degree by the repeated usurpation of Maximus, but in reality the four disparate tribes were not in any position to have Maximus formally recognized in Rome.

In addition, although it is implied in the ancient sources that the Alans were the leaders of a four-tribe confederation, there is no practical evidence for the claim. It is possible that the Silings and the Alans were allied in support of Maximus, but there is no indication that the Asdings or the Sueves were involved at this time. The decision to use the Goths against the tribes in Hispania resulted in three of the tribes coalescing to form a far more dangerous entity which, although they remained far too weak to threaten Rome and Italy, were strong enough to repulse a major Roman campaign that attempted to defeat them.

It is, however, possible even here to defend his actions. It is quite likely that at some point he intended to follow the Gothic attacks and himself lead an army to the peninsula in order to finally solve the problem of the four tribes, either by defeating them and settling the survivors on Roman terms or simply by a mass extermination. That his unexpected death prevented this happening is not something he could have foreseen. Of more importance, nobody at the time could have predicted that the new coalition in Hispania would come to be led by the most intelligent, able and charismatic leader any of the barbarian tribes would ever have: Gaiseric.[52]

More than any other barbarian – even the famous Attila the Hun – it was Gaiseric whose actions helped to weaken the West to the point where its very survival was open to question. The loss of the grain and the revenue from Africa was to prove disastrous for Rome, but when he died in 421 Constantius did not know of these future events. It is even possible that, had he lived, a major campaign in Hispania could have eliminated Gunderic and Gaiseric and so ensured the continued loyalty of Africa far into the future. However, that is to revert to extreme speculation: all that needs to be noted here is that Constantius' future plans were unknown when he died, but his previous military campaigns had usually resulted in success so anything would have been possible.

There then remains the question of whether Constantius was really planning a campaign against the Eastern Empire in order to confirm his position as *Augustus*, or whether this was to be a campaign aimed at reclaiming the Illyrian recruiting grounds. As Theodosius' preparations in the East had resulted in a war with Sasanid Persia, it is feasible that Theodosius would have acceded to Constantius' demands and simply returned Illyricum, a region in which the East had no long-term vested interest after the defeat of the Goths in 382. With the ability to reinforce his army with quality new recruits, what Constantius would have been able to achieve is open to question, but it is likely that the Vandal invasion of Africa would not have occurred.

Bearing these deductions in mind, it is possible to suggest that, had Constantius lived, his strategic and political ability may have fundamentally altered the future of the Western Roman Empire and enabled it to continue far into the future. As such, it is further possible to suggest that he was indeed Rome's Lost Hope.

Notes

Acknowledgements
1. Hughes, 2017.
2. Hughes, 2019.
3. Hughes, 2010.
4. Hughes, 2012.
5. Hughes, 2015.

Introduction
1. Heather, 1994, 5f.
2. For the Chronicles of Prosper and Hydatius and the *Gallic Chronicle of 452* and *511* Muhlberger is an invaluable introduction and commentary, from which much of this section is derived.
3. Muhlberger, 2006, 2.
4. Muhlberger, 2006, 147.
5. Whitby and Whitby, 1989, ix.
6. Muhlberger, 2006, 147; 213.
7. Muhlberger, 2006, 213.
8. Halsall, 2007, 237. n.78.
9. Oost, 1964, 23.
10. Wood, in CAH, 519–520.
11. *Cod. Th.* 1.1.5 (26 March 429).
12. Freeman, 1887, 423.
13. E.g. Gaiseric being spelled 'Zinzirich', *Chron. Pasch.* s.a. 439.
14. Kulikowski, 2002, 69, n.2.
15. Collins, 2006, 19.

Chapter One
1. Matthews, 1998, 319–20.
2. For a summary of current thinking, O'Flynn, 1983, 15. On Stilicho, see Greg. Tur. 2.8 (*a puero praetorianus*): c.f. PLRE I and II, *Stilicho.*
3. *Cod. Just.* 12.23; description of the post, Blume, 2009, 12.23 (p.9). See also Jones, 1973, Vol. 2, 174, n.67.
4. Jones, 1973, 200.
5. Jones, 1973, 139.
6. Jones, 1973, 140f.

7. A similar system was adopted by Adolf Hitler in Germany between 1933 and 1945. The main purpose appears to have been to encourage friction between individuals, resulting in there being less chance of these same men allying with each other to overthrow Hitler. Although unattested, it is possible that the emperors followed this tradition as a matter of policy rather than of mere chance.

8. For a more detailed discussion of the *Notitia*, see the Introduction.

9. Jones, 1973, 173.

10. A good example of this followed Stilicho's war against Gildo in 398. When Stilicho seized Gildo's lands for the Empire following his victory, they were so great that a new official, the *Comes Gildoniaci Patrimonii* (Count of the Patrimony of Gildo), had to be appointed to administer them: Hughes, 2010, 112: Zos. 5.13.4.

11. Rouche, 1989, 29–31.

12. Rouche, 1989, 31.

13. Rouche, 1989, 34–35.

14. These laws appear to have been introduced by Diocletian in the hope of solving internal problems of recruitment, training and social mobility. C.f. Fossier, 1989, 8.

15. For a more detailed examination of the cause and effect of these changes, Hughes, 2010, 151–52.

16. Fossier, 1989, 8.

17. Thompson, 1952, 1506.

18. C.f. Halsall, 2007, 249, where he notes that the *bacaudae* in Spain were 'local landlords who had established their own authority'.

Chapter Two

1. Much of the information in this chapter was previously covered in Hughes, 2010, Chapter 6.

2. E.g. Zos., 4. 58. 2.

3. Cameron, 1970, 60.

4. Zos., 4. 59. The omission of Britain appears to be a mistake on the part of Zosimus.

5. Alaric's reward; Soc. 7.10 where he is 'honoured with Roman dignities', the most obvious being given the title *Comes militaris*: wanting regular forces to command, Zos., 5.5.4.

6. Liebeschuetz claims that Alaric and Rufinus came to an agreement and that Alaric and his followers were settled in Thessaly prior to the arrival of Stilicho with the army (1998, 58).

7. Claud. in *Ruf.* II, 186–96.

8. Cameron, 1990, 86.

9. Claud., *Bell. Get.*, 516f.

10. Claudian later attempted to annul the declaration by claiming that Stilicho had gone to Greece on the orders of Honorius: IV *Cons. Hon.*, 459f. See also Cameron, 1970, 96f.

11. Claud., *de Cons. Stil.* I, 314f: II, 393f; III, 91f, and *In. Eut.* I, 401f.
12. For a detailed description of the earlier form of *senatus consultum*, see 'Smith's Dictionary of Greek and Roman Antiquities' at http://penelope.uchicago.edu/Thayer/E/Roman/Texts/secondary/SMIGRA*/Senatusconsultum.html
13. C.f. Millar, 1982, 4f.
14. Claud. *In. Eut.* II, 214–18.
15. *Not. Dig.*, *Or.*, xi, 35–9. Horreum Margi, possibly to be identified as Požarevac in Serbia.
16. On the date, Cameron, 1970, 109.
17. Liebeschuetz, 1998, 62; Claud., *de Bello Get.*, 568; Soz. 9. 6.
18. Some historians date the invasion to 400, following the ancient chronicles such as Prosper, *Prosperi Tironis epitome chronicon* (*Chronicon Minores* I, 341–485) and Cassiodorus, *Cassiodori Senatoris Chronica* (*Chronicon Minores* II, 111–61). This assumes that the chronicles are correct concerning the date of the Raetian invasion, but are incorrect in assuming that Alaric was involved. It is clear that Stilicho led a winter campaign against the Vandals and it is also certain that Alaric invaded in late autumn 401. Yet the sources claim that the passes into Italy were unguarded and this is most likely the result of troops being withdrawn for the Raetian campaign. If Stilicho's campaign in Raetia had been in 400–401, it is likely that by autumn of 401 at least some of the troops would have been returned to guard the passes into Italy. Therefore, it is more likely that Stilicho's campaign began in early autumn 401 and that Alaric's invasion was partly based on the knowledge that Stilicho had been called away with the army. This assumes that the sources have confused the date by one year and assumed that Alaric was involved in any barbarian invasion of the West.
19. On the campaign being in winter, Claud., *de Bell. Get.*, 348–9.
20. Claud., *de Bello Get.*, 151–3 (in Italy one winter prior to the Battle of Pollentia in 402); *Chron. Min.*, I, 299.
21. Jerome, *Apologeticum adversus Rufinum* at http://www.newadvent.org/fathers/27103.htm (December 2008).
22. Claud., *de Bello Getico*, 278f.
23. Claud., *de VI Cons. Hon.*, 454f.
24. The first law issued from Ravenna is dated 6 December 402. *Cod. Th.*, 7.13.15.
25. Claud., *de Bello Getico*, 623f.
26. Retiring with the majority of his cavalry intact, Claud., *VI Cons. Hon.*, 274f; Camp and booty captured, *de Bello Getico*, 605f, 624f.
27. On the negotiations, Claud., *VI Cons. Hon.* 210; abandon Italy, *de Bello Get.*, 144; *VI Cons. Hon.*, 138. The passage at *de Bello Get.* 646–8 implies that the invasion is now over. See Liebeschuetz, 2004, 63. I disagree with Cameron (1970, 181) and Wolfram (1990, 152) who see the claim as fictitious and an attempt by Claudian to protect Stilicho from claims of treason and incompetence, and suggest instead that he was in an alliance with Alaric.

28. O'Flynn, 1983, 40.
29. O'Flynn, 1983, 41.
30. Claud., *de VI Cons. Hon.*, 239–44.
31. Sarus, *PLRE* II, 978; Segericus *PLRE* II, 987.
32. Halsall, 2007, 202.
33. Soz., 8.25.3–4; 9.4.2–4.
34. On dating the hostage exchange, which included Aetius, later *magister militum* himself, to 402 rather than 405, Liebeschuetz, 1998, 63–4; Halsall, 2007, 202.
35. *Dux Pannoniae Secundae* = *Not. Dig.* Oc. I, 40. On the location of the settlement, Soz., 8.25.3–4; IX 4.4. On the title of 'King of the Goths' and 'Count of the Romans', *Not. Dig. Or.* 2.3.3. See Cameron, 1970, 185 for a discussion of these events. On the earlier appointments of a *Comes rei militaris* of Africa see Chapter 8 and of Britain see Chapter 9.
36. For the complexities surrounding this event, Williams and Friell, 1994, 155; on the date, 223, note 52; see also Heather, 1994, 221.
37. 'Seeing that Arcadius' ministers were alienated from him', Zos.,8.26.1–2.
38. It is possible that Stilicho 'revived or manufactured a claim' that Theodosius had ordered that the prefecture of Illyricum be attached to the West; CAH, 2004, 121.
39. Rutilius Namatianus, *de Reditu suo*, 41f: http://penelope.uchicago.edu/Thayer/E/Roman/Texts/Rutilius_Namatianus/text*.html (July 2009).
40. '400,000 Gauls and Germans', Zos., 5.26.3. For a more believable estimation of numbers, see the discussion in Hughes, 2010, 164.
41. Oros., 7.37.2; Marc. *com.* s.a. 406; Jord. *Rom.*, 321; c.f. Hughes, 2019, 61.
42. Williams and Friell, 1995, 155.
43. Soz., 8.25.
44. Soz., 8.25; Zos., 5.27.2.
45. Zos., 5.27.2.
46. For a more detailed analysis of these events, see Hughes, 2010, 177f.
47. *Chron. Gall. 452*, s.a. 442.
48. Roymans, 2017, 68.
49. Olymp. fr. 12, perhaps giving the date as late 406; c.f. *PLRE* 2, *Marcus* 2, 719; Zos., 6.2.1, giving the date as 407; c.f. Soz., 9.11.2; Oros., 7.40.4.
50. Dating: Burns, 1994, 210; reason for overthrow, Kulikowski, 2000, 332.
51. For a full itinerary of the cities attacked, see Hughes, 2010, 183–84.
52. We are not informed directly that Constantine attempted to ally himself with the Vandals, Sueves and Alans. However, Oros. 7.40.4 and 7. 28. describes 'unreliable alliances' with barbarians and how these treaties were 'not strictly kept'. This can only relate to treaties with the invaders.
53. Oros., 7.28.
54. CAH, 2004, 129; c.f. Roymans, 2017, 68.
55. Oros., 7.40.5.
56. Zos., 5.27.2.

57. On the divisions in the Senate, see Ribeiro Machado, 2013, 55f.
58. As a reward for his service, Heraclianus was made *Comes Africae*: Zos., 5.37.6; *PLRE* 2, *Heraclianus* 3, 539. He remained loyal to Honorius and was granted the consulship in 413. In that same year he rebelled, aiming to become emperor, before being murdered.
59. Zos., 5.34.4. For the date of the execution, *Addit. Ad Prosp. Haun.*, s.a. 408.
60. Zos., 5.34.5.
61. Zos., 5.37.6.

Chapter Three
 1. Zos., 5.35.1; Philost., 12.1; Olymp. frg. 8.
 2. *CTh.*, 9.42.22.
 3. Zos., 5.35.3.
 4. Zos., 5.37.6.
 5. Zos., 5.35.6; 40,000 men, 5.42.3.
 6. See Chapter 11: Heather, 1994, 213f.
 7. Zos., 5.36.1.
 8. Dunn, 2010, 248–49.
 9. Zos., 5.36. For a more detailed analysis of Sarus' career, see Wijnendaele, J.W.P., 'Sarus the Goth: From Imperial Commander to Warlord', *Early Medieval Europe*, 2019 27 (4), pp.469–93.
10. Zos., 1.16.
11. Zos., 5.36.3. Turpilio and Vigilantius were both killed following a mutiny of the troops in March 409, but Varanes was made consul in the East in 410; Ridley, 1983, 220, n. 132–34.
12. Zos., 5–37.
13. Zos., 5.37.1; Hodgkin, 1892, 766; October, e.g. Wolfram, 1990, 155–56.
14. Wolfram, 1990, 155.
15. C.f. Burns, 1994, 227.
16. Zos., 5.37.2f.
17. Zos., 5.37.2–4.
18. This question is raised by Burns (1994, p.228) without a satisfactory conclusion being reached.
19. Soc., 7.10. The vague account of Socrates means that this alleged meeting could be dated anywhere between 408 and 410.
20. Dunn, 2009, 325.
21. Zos., 5.38–39.
22. Heather, 1994, 215.
23. C.f. Geront., *Vita Mel.* 19.
24. Soz., 9.6.5–6; Zos., 5.41.1–3.
25. J. Norwich, *Byzantium: The Early Centuries*, 134.
26. This John may be the same man who later usurped the throne and was supported by Aetius: Hodgkin, 1892, 768.
27. Zos., 5.44.1.

28. Zos., 5.44.2.
29. Zos., 5.50.1; c.f. 5.46.6; Hughes, 2019, 63.
30. Greg. Tur., 2.8; Merob. *Pan.* 2.1–4.
31. Hughes, 2019, 67.
32. Zos., 5.37.1.
33. Zos., 5.45.4–5. Sozomen claims that only Innocent was sent to Ravenna: Soz., 9.7.1.
34. Dunn, 2010, 258.
35. Zos., 6.5.2; Prosp. s.a. 411; Greg. Tur., 2.9; Olymp. frg. 17.1; Oros. 7.42.4 dated to after the death of Constans in 411; Soz., 9.13.1.
36. Constans was 'worsted in battle', *CAH*, 1998, 129.
37. Zos., 6.5.2.
38. Jer. *Ep.* 123.16; Kulikowski, 2000, 331.
39. Zos., 5.46.1.

Chapter Four

1. The precise chronology of events in this year is confused and open to widely differing interpretations. What follows is only one hypothesis. Others also exist and some of these are mentioned in the endnotes.
2. Jovius retained close ties with Alaric, Zos., 5.48.2; Soz., 9.4.4; meeting, Soz., 9.7.1.
3. Zos., 5.38–44.
4. Zos., 48.3.
5. Zos., 48.4.
6. Zos., 5.49.1; 9.7.4.
7. Zos., 5.45–52; Soz., 9.7.
8. C.f. Wolfram, 1990, 157.
9. It would appear that there were two distinct individuals named Valens who occupied important military posts at this time. The one here is the Valens named by Zosimus as being the general of the troops withdrawn from Dalmatia to garrison Rome. He then remained in Rome and was promoted to a higher military command under Attalus. The second Valens is described as being in Ravenna and was a close associate of Jovius. c.f. *PLRE* 2, *Valens* 1 and *Valens* 2, pp.1136–7. He is recorded as accompanying Jovius on an embassy to Attalus and Alaric after the first Valens had already accepted a post in Attalus' regime.
10. Zos., 5.45.1.
11. See Chapter 6.
12. *CTh.* 16.5.42 (14 November 408, Ravenna). 'Within the Palace' may mean as part of the *Palatina*.
13. C.f. *PLRE* 2, Generidus, pp.500–501.
14. Praise, Zos., 5.46.2; free from incursions, Zos., 5.46.5.
15. Zos., 5.49 – 6.1; Date, Dunn, 2009, 325.
16. Rut. Nam. *De Red.* 325f; Matthews, 1975, 352.

17. C.f. Phil. 12.3; Olymp. frg. 14.
18. C.f. Dunn, 2009, 325.
19. Elton, 1999, has a different chronology, in which the barbarian invasion of Hispania comes before Gerontius' rebellion.
20. Zos., 6.5.2.
21. This model is rejected by some historians: e.g. Halsall, 2007, 227.
22. C.f. Phil., 12.3; Olymp. frg. 14.
23. C.f. Philost. 12; Olymp. frg. 14.
24. Zos., 6.12.3.
25. Zos., 6.7.5; 8.3; 6.10.2.
26. C.f. Ribeiro Machado, 2014, 58.
27. C.f. Ribeiro Machado, 2014, 56.
28. On Gaiseric, see Hughes, 2017, *passim*.
29. Constans, Soz., 9.8.12–22; Zos., 6.7.5–6; Battle, c.f. Oros., 7.42.10.
30. Zos., 6.10.2; grain, Zos., 6.11.
31. Olymp. frg. 14.
32. C.f. *CAH*, 2004, 217, n.19; c.f. Zos., 5.30.4–5; 31.3–6; 31.48.4; 6.8.1.3.
33. Olymp. frg.13.
34. Olymp. frg. 14.
35. Olymp. frg. 13/14; Zos., 6.8.1.
36. Olymp. frg. 13.
37. Olymp. frg. 14.
38. Zos., 6.13.1; Soz., 9.12.4ff; Olymp. frg. 16.
39. *CAH*, 2004, 127.
40. Soz., 9.8.6; Zos., 6.8.2; c.f. Proc. *BV.* 1.2.36.
41. C.f. McEvoy, 2014, *passim*.
42. Zos., 6.8.
43. Olymp. frg. 14; Soz., 9.12.5.

Chapter Five
1. The precise chronology of events in this year is confused and open to widely differing interpretations. What follows is only one hypothesis. Others also exist and some of these are mentioned in the endnotes.
2. Constantius is claimed by Theophanes (AM 5895) to have been a *comes* alongside Alaric and to have fled with Placidia in 402/3. This is recorded nowhere else and is here dismissed.
3. C.f. Burns, 1994, 243.
4. On these and other hypotheses, see *CAH*, 2004, 129.
5. Soz., 9.12.4.
6. Soc., 7.10.
7. Olymp. frg. 10.48–53; Philost., 12.3.
8. Olymp. frg. 13; Zos., 6.9.1–3, 2–12.
9. Zos., 6.6–12; Soz., 9.7.
10. C.f. Fabbro, 2015, 51.

11. Date, Prosp. *Chron. Min.* 1240; Theoph. *AM* 5903; Zos., 6.13; Soz., 9.9. Three days, Oros., 7.38.15; Six days, Marc. *com.* s.a. 410.
12. Among others, Gelens, 2014, and Dunn, 2009, provide a useful collection and analysis of the sources.
13. Proc. *BV.* 1.2.
14. Proc. *BV.* 1.2.27.
15. C.f. Salzman, 2009, 175; Salzman, 2013, 295f.
16. There are five sources of length on the sack: Orosius (Western, wr. c.417); Socrates (Eastern, wr. c.440); Sozomen (Eastern, wr. c.440); Zosimus (Eastern, wr. second-half fifth century); and Procopius (Eastern, wr. mid-sixth century), plus several shorter notices. On these, see esp. Mathisen, 2013, *passim.*
17. Salzman, 2009, 175.
18. Philost., 12.3.
19. A theory adopted by some modern historians: e.g. Bury, *Italy and Her Invaders*, p.64; c.f. Costa, 2007, 60.
20. Gelens, 2014, 16.
21. 'Terrible time of massacre', Aug., *De Civ. Dei* 1.1 2; 'Destructions, fires, acts of rapine, killings, torturing of men', Aug. *Exc. Urb* 3.
22. Phil., 12.3; Soc., 7.10.4. c.f. Soz., 9.9; Olymp. frg. 26; Jord. *Rom.* 43; Hyd. s.a. 410; Jer. *Ep.* 127, 12; Proc. *BV.* 1.2; Aug. *Civ.* 1.28; Oros., 7.39; Marc. *com.* s.a. 410.
23. Churches sacked, Jer., *Ep.* 128.5.
24. Oros., 7.39.
25. 'St. Peter's', Soz., 9.9.4; 'limited sack', Soz., 9.10.
26. Oros., 7.39.1–40.20; C.f. Olymp. frg. 20.1–3; 22.1–3; 24.
27. Oros., 7.39.
28. Jord., 30.156; Isid. *Hist. Goth.* 15.
29. Leo., *Serm.* 84.1.
30. Brown, 1961, 3–10; Fabbro, 2015, 51.
31. Mathisen, 2013, 93. C.f. *PLRE 2, Alaric*, pp.43–8.

Chapter Six
1. Soc., 7.10.
2. Hyd., s.a. 410; Marc., *com.* s.a. 410; Jord. *Rom.* 43; Olymp. frg. 23.
3. Inn. I, *Ep.* 16.
4. C.f. Ribeiro Machado, 2014, 56, 59.
5. Dunn, 2009, 331.
6. http://www.vortigernstudies.org.uk/artsou/zosim.htm
7. For more on the rescript, see e.g. Wood, 2012, *passim*; Halsall, 2007, 217.
8. Zos., 6.5.3, c.f. 6.10; Jones, 1973, 187.
9. C.f. Thompson, 1982, 50.
10. Aug. *Civ. Dei* 1.10; Philost. 12.3; Jord. *Get.* 156.
11. Olymp. frg. 15; Oros., 7.43.2; Jord. *Get.* 156.

12. Olymp. frg. 15; Oros., 7.43.2; Jord. *Get.* 156.
13. Olymp. frg. 10; Hyd., 45; Philost., 12.3; Jord. *Get.* 156–8; Proc. *BV.* 1.2.37.
14. Jord. *Get.* 158.
15. Hyd., 45; Olymp. frg. 10; Oros., 7.43.2; *Chron. Gall. 452* no. 69; Jord. *Get.* 158.
16. Roymans, 2017, 68.
17. Hyd., s.a. 411.
18. Olymp. frg. 16; Soz., 9.13.1.
19. Prosp., s.a. 411; cavalry commander, Soz., 9.14.2.
20. 10,000 Huns, Zosimus, 5.50; contra, e.g. *PLRE* 2, *Vlphilas*, p.1181, where he is assumed to be either *magister equitum in praesenti* or *magister equitum per Gallias*. See also Chapter 4.
21. 4,000 Eastern troops, Soz., 9.8.6; Zos., 6.8.2; c.f. Proc. *BV.* 1.2.36; see Chapter 4.
22. Olymp. frg. 16; c.f. Soz., 9.14.
23. Matthews, 1998, 331. Oros., 7. 43. A complex and debatable passage in Orosius also implies that a peace treaty had been concluded, although no date is given; Oros., 7.43.
24. Kulikowski, 2001, 28; Hydatius, *passim*, but c.f. Oros., 7.41.7.
25. Collins, 2006, 15.
26. Attacks from 'beyond the Rhine', Zos., 6.5–6; attack by Saxons, *Chron. Gall. 452*, no. 62.
27. Zos., 6.5–6; 'Now the defection of Britannia and the Celtic peoples took place during Constantine's tyranny.'
28. Greg. Tur. 2.9; Soz., 9.13.2.
29. See Olymp. frg. 17.2 for the main story of the ambush and the result.
30. Soz., 9.14.
31. Olymp. frg. 17; Greg. Tur. 2.9; c.f. Oros., 7.42.6; Soz., 9.15.3; Prosp., s.a. 413.
32. Drinkwater, 2007, 325.
33. C.f. Matthews, 1975, 314.
34. Greg. Tur. 2.9; c.f. Oros., 7.46.2; Soz., 9. 15.3; Philost., 12. 6; Prosp., s.a.413; Hyd. 51 (a. 412).
35. Prosp., s.a. 413.
36. Fred. *Chron.* 3.7; discussion in Mathisen, 1993, 77.
37. Roymans, 2016, 68.
38. Roymans, 2017, 69.
39. Soz., 9.15.1.
40. Olymp. frg. 16; Soz., 9.15.1; Oros., 7.42.2; Prosp., s.a. 411; *Addit. Ad Prosp. Haun.* s.a. 411; *Chron. Gall. 452* s.a. 410; Hyd. a. 411; Marc. *com.* s.a. 411; Greg. Tur., 2.9; Jord. *Get.* 165; Jord. *Rom.* 324; Theoph. *AM* 5903; c.f. *CAH*, 130.
41. Date, *Cons. Const.* s.a. 411; Olymp. frg. 19.
42. Olymp. frg. 16; Soz., 9.15.1; *Chron. Min.* 1.466 (Prosper).

43. C.f. *CAH* 130.
44. Renatus Profuturus Frigeridus = Greg. Tur., 2.9.
45. Halsall, 2007, 218.
46. Matthews, 1998, 354–6, 382.
47. See Chapter 2.
48. On later events, see esp. Hughes, 2012, 2015, *passim*.
49. Jord. *Get.* 159; *CTh.* 9.28.7 (8 May 412); Rut. Nam. *De reditu suo sive* 1.21; C.f. *CTh.* 11.28.12 (15 November 418), showing the severe level of damage caused by the Goths.
50. Matthews, 1998, 331. Oros., 7.43. As noted above, a complex and debatable passage in Orosius also implies that a peace treaty had been concluded, although no date is given; Oros. 7.43.
51. Kulikowski, 2001, 28; Hydatius, *passim*, but c.f. Oros., 7.41.7.
52. Collins, 2006, 15.
53. Jovinus minting coins, Halsall, 2007, 223 citing Cesa, M., *Impero Tardoantico e Barbari: La Crisi Militare de da Adrianopoli al 418* (Como, 1994).
54. Olymp. frg. 18; c.f. Soz., 9.15.3.
55. Wolfram, 1990, 162; c.f. *CTh.* 9.28.7 (8 May 412).
56. Rut. Nam. *De Red. Suo* 1, esp. 21f; Matthews, 1975, 325.
57. Olymp. frg. 17.
58. Olymp. frg. 18.
59. Olymp. frg. 201.1.
60. Olymp. frg. 18, 20. There is no mention of any other condition in the agreement: c.f. Heather, 1991, 219.
61. Although not mentioned directly at this point, Olympiodorus implies that the return of Galla was one of the conditions; frg. 22.1.
62. Philost., 12.1.
63. E.g. *Chron. Gall. 452* a. 414.
64. *CAH*, 131; c.f. Prosp. s.a. 413.
65. *Chron. Gall. 452*, s.a. 19 [71].
66. Olymp. frg. 20–21; Hyd. 19 (46 [54]) s.a. 413; Oros., 7.42.6; Jord. *Get.* 165; Theoph. *AM* 5904.
67. Sid. Ap. *Ep.* 5.9.1.
68. Wijnendaele, 2017, 141; C.f. Zos., 5.37.6.
69. *CTh.* 7.18.17 (29 February 412, Ravenna).
70. Usurper, Jer. *Adv. Pelag.* 3.19; In *Ezech.*, 9.28; Olymp. frg. 23; Prosp. s.a. 413; *Chron. Gall. 452*, 75; Hyd. 43 [51].
71. *CTh.* 9.40.21 (3 August 413, Ravenna).
72. On these assumptions, see esp. Wijnendaele, 2017, 146–7; 2020.
73. On these events, see Hughes, 2012, 57–74.
74. Oros., 7.42.12–13.
75. C.f. Wijnendaele, 2017, 149.
76. Oros., 7.42.12–14; Hyd. 19 (48[56]) s.a. 413. Hydatius claims that his army suffered 50,000 casualties in the battle, but this number is certainly far too high.

77. Date, *Rav. Ann.* Col. 1, 7–8; *CTh.* 9.40.21, 15.14.13 (both 3 August 413, Ravenna); Olymp. frg. 23; Hyd. 48[56]; *Chron. Gall. 452*, 20[75].
78. Olymp. frg. 23.
79. Narbonne, Hyd. 19 (47[55]) s.a. 413.

Chapter Seven
1. Olymp. frg. 22.2.
2. *Olymp. frg. 22.2; c.f. Oost, 1968, 124.*
3. East, e.g. Kelly, 2008, 53; West, e.g. Maenchen-Helfen, 1973, 73–4; based upon Olymp. frg. 18.
4. Fasti, 414; Olymp. frg. 23; *AE* 194.5, 133; In *Ep.* 17; c.f. *CTh.* 7.4.34 (19 November 414).
5. Olymp. frg. 22.2.
6. Olymp. frg. 22.3.
7. Olymp. frg. 24; c.f. Goldsworthy, 2009, 303.
8. E.g. Hyd., 49 [57], a. 414; Philost., 12.4; Forum Julii, Jord. *Get.* 131/160.
9. Oros., 7.43.2–3; but c.f. Heather, 1991, 219.
10. Pawluk, 2005, 225. It should be noted that the omission may in part at least be due to her not being designated as *Augusta*.
11. Paul. Pell., *Euch.* 312–14; Rut. Nam., *Itin.* 1.496.
12. Jord., *Get.* 164; Oros., 7.43.1; Hyd., 60; Amidon, 2007, pp.157–8, n.14.
13. Prosp., s.a. 414.
14. Hyd., 2 [60], a. 416; sack, Paul. Pell., *Thanksgiving*, p.254.
15. Prosp., s.a. 415.
16. Oros., 7.42.9; Prosp., s.a. 415.
17. Olymp. frg. 17, 19–21; Oros., 7.43.1; *Paul. Pell., Euch. 377–85; Prisc. frg. 49; Soz., 9.5.1–5.*
18. Olymp. frg. 26.1; c.f. Hyd., 57.
19. Heather, 1991, 220.
20. Halsall, 2007, 226.
21. Olymp. frg. 26.
22. C.f. Prosp., s.a. 415; *CTh.* 15.14.14 (1 March 416); Hyd., 60, a. 416.
23. Olymp. frg. 20, 22, 26.
24. Jones, 1964, 187–8.
25. For a more detailed analysis of affairs in Hispania between 409 and 416, see Latham-Sprinkle, 2012, *passim*.
26. Hyd., *Cont.* 68; c.f. Sid. Ap., *Carm.* 2, 362–5. On the economy, see Latham-Sprinkle, 2012, referencing also Fernando Lopez Sanchez, 'Coinage, Iconography and the Changing Political Geography of 5th-Century Hispania' in Bowes & Kulikowski, *Hispania*, 497, 505–506 and Paul Reynolds, 'Hispania in the Late Roman Mediterranean: Ceramics and Trade' in Bowes & Kulikowski, *Hispania*, 392.
27. Oros., 7.43.13–14.
28. Kulikowski, 2001, 28; Hydatius, *passim*, but c.f. Oros., 7.41.7.
29. Collins, 2006, 15.

30. This is equivalent to 48 *solidi* per *modius* of grain, whereas the standard rate was 40 *modii* of grain per *solidus*; Blockley, 1983, 218, n. 62.
31. Halsall, 2007, 226.
32. Jord., *Get.* 163; c.f. Isid. Sev., *Hist.* 22.
33. Oros., 7.43.15–16.
34. Jord., *Get.* 163; Olymp. frg. 26.1.13f; c.f. Oros., 7.43.2.8; Philost., 12.4; Prosp., s.a. 415; Hyd., 52 [60] s.a. 414, who merely claims the perpetrator was a Goth.
35. Olymp. frg. 26.1.13f.
36. Oros., 7.43.9.
37. Jord., *Get.* 163; c.f. Oros., 7.9; Olymp. frg. 26.1.13f.
38. Prosp., s.a. 415; Oros. 7.43.10.

Chapter Eight

1. *Chron. Gall. 452*, 78, a. 416.
2. Oros., 7.42; clearly only one 'band' (*manus*); Philost., 12.4–5; Halsall, 2007, 226; c.f. Heather, 1999, 97.
3. E.g. Heather, 1994, 221.
4. C.f. Oros., 7.43.5f; Elton, 2004, 11.
5. Olymp. frg. 30.
6. Olymp. frg. 13; c.f. Philost., 12.5.
7. C.f. *CTh.* 15.14.14 (1 March 416).
8. Oros., 7.43.10–13; Hyd., 60; c.f. Jord., *Get.* 164ff.
9. C.f. Olymp. frg. 29.1, 30; Philost., 12.4.5; Oros., 7.43.10ff; Prosp., s.a. 416; *Chron. Gall. 452*, a. 416 (21–22/77); Hyd., 60; c.f. Jord., *Get.* 164ff; probably *foederati*, e.g. Jones, 1964, 188.
10. Heather, 1994, 221.
11. Olymp. frg. 30; c.f. Jones, 1964, 188.
12. Jord., *Get.*, 164–66.
13. Oros., 7.43.
14. C.f. *Chron. Gall. 452*, 27/85, a. 416.
15. But c.f. Burns, 2002, 55.
16. For a more detailed analysis of the events in 418, see Latham-Sprinkle, 2012, *passim.*
17. C.f. Garnica, 1999, 97.
18. See esp. Latham-Sprinkle, 2012.
19. Sid. Ap., *Carm.* 2, 362–5, in Alemany, A., *Sources on the Alans: A Critical Companion* (Leiden, 2000), 72–3.

Chapter Nine

1. A good starting-point for analysis of the problems surrounding the Gothic settlement is Goffart, 1980, pp.103–126.
2. Burns, 2002, 60.
3. Zos., 5.50.3.

4. C.f. Heather, 1994, 223–4.
5. Garnica, 1999, 97.
6. For a more detailed discussion, see Burns, 2002, 62f and Bibliography.
7. Especially important in this context, Schwarcz, 2011, *passim*.
8. E.g. Schwarcz, 2011, 267.
9. Schwarcz, 2001, 268–9.
10. Philost., 12.4.
11. Nixon, 2002, 72.
12. As described in the *Visigothic Code of Euric*, Bury, 1923, 206. n. 89; Goffart, 1980, 109f.
13. Nixon, 2002, 70; Goths needing land to farm, c.f. *AM* 31.3.1,8; 31.4.5,8; 31.9.4; 31.12.8.
14. Diaz, 1999, 327.
15. C.f. Garnica, 1999, 104.
16. Diaz, 1999, 323.
17. C.f. Garnica, 1999, 104.
18. Goffart, 1980, 112; Nixon, 2002, 70; c.f. *Pan. Lat.* 8(4).21.297.
19. Schwarcz, 2011, 267.
20. Olymp. frg. 8; *PLRE* 2, Constantius, 17, 322.
21. Thompson, 1982, 52.
22. Thompson, 1982, 52.
23. 418, Hyd., 69–70, s.a. 418; c.f. Olymp. frg. 34; Philost., 12.4; 419, Prosp., 1271, s.a. 419. In a modern example, the date of 419 is used by Schwarcz in Mathisen and Shanzer, 2011, 15–25.
24. C.f. Nixon, 2002, 71.
25. Garnica, 1999, 97.
26. E.g. sid. ap. *Carm.* 7.469; *Ep.* 7.6.4.
27. Nixon, 2002, 71.
28. Burns, 2002, 62.
29. Fred., *Chron.* MGH SRM 2. 71, lines 26–7.
30. Wolfram, 1990, 173.
31. Jones, 1966, 68.
32. Jones, 1966, 81f; c.f. Bury, 1923, Vol. 1, 207.
33. Nixon, 2002, 71.
34. C.f. Wolfram, 1990, 174.
35. C.f. Burns, 2002, 57.
36. C.f. Garnica, 1999, 96.
37. C.f. Matthews, 1975, 322.
38. Jones, 1973, 81.
39. Halsall, 2007, 231.
40. Ward-Perkins, 2006, 56, referencing A. Loyen, '*Les Débuts du royaume wisigoth de Toulouse*', *Revue des études latines*, 12 (1934), 406–15.
41. Ward-Perkins, 2006, 67.
42. Philost., 12.4; c.f. Wolfram, 1990, 173; friction, e.g. Matthews, 1975, 330.

43. Ward-Perkins, 2006, 66.
44. Fossier, 1989, 53.
45. Diaz, 1999, 331.
46. Hyd., s.a. 418.
47. Collins, 2006, 25, referencing Courtois, *Les Vandales*, Paris, 1955, 229.
48. Poss., 28.
49. Heather, 2005, 264–5.
50. Zos., 5.48.3.
51. C.f. Heather, 2005, 223.
52. *PLRE* 2, *Theodericus* 2, 10170; cf. sid. ap. *Carm.* 7.505.
53. Sid. ap. *Carm.* 7. 505. Theoderic is nowhere mentioned as Alaric's son, and since Sidonius attests that Theoderic's son, also called Theoderic, was the grandson of Alaric, Theoderic must have married Alaric's daughter.

Chapter Ten

1. Olymp. frg. 33.1; Hyd., 54(62).
2. Olymp. frg. 30.
3. Marcell., *com.* s.a. 419; Theoph. *AM* 5912; c.f. *AM* 5911. Hydatius (63(71)) dates the birth to 419.
4. Olymp. frg. 37.
5. *CAH*, 132.
6. E.g. Gildas, *De Excid.* 23; c.f. Morris, 2001, 43ff, esp. 45.
7. Morris, 2001, 44.
8. Morris, 2001, 44–5.
9. *CAH*, 133.
10. Matthews, 1975, 333.
11. Rut. Nam., *De Red. Suo*, 1.213–16, pp.226–7; Philost. 12.4.
12. Burns, 2002, 60.
13. C.f. Halsall, 2007, 233–4.
14. Maier, 2012, 67–8.
15. *Epistolae Arelatenses* 8; Wolfram, 1990, 173; Schwarcz, 2011, 268; Mathisen, 1993, 19.
16. But c.f. *CAH*, 133.
17. Halsall, 2007, 231.
18. C.f. *CAH*, 133.
19. Halsall, 2007, 231; c.f. *Querolus* 2 (29–34).
20. Halsall, 2007, 232.
21. Halsall, 2007, 232.
22. Matthews, 1975, 336.
23. Ward-Perkins, 2006, 70.
24. Fossier, 1989, 53.
25. Prosp., s.a. 418; Theoph. *AM* 5911, 5912.
26. Thompson, 1982, 52–3.
27. Hyd., 62(70).
28. Thompson, 1982, 53.

29. *Leges Visig.* 3.1.2.
30. C.f. Nixon, 2002, 65.
31. Hyd., 63(71); Halsall, 2007, 233.
32. Prosp., s.a. 419.
33. *Parens principium*; *PLRE* 2, *Constantius* 17.323, *Inscr.* 1–2; Emperor, *PLRE* 2, *Constantius* 17, 324; Theoph. *AM* 5913; Placidia *Augusta*, Olymp. frg. 31; Prosp., s.a. 423, 425; Valentinian *nobilissimus*; Olymp. frg. 34; Philost., 12.12.
34. Ren. Prof. Frig. Date, Halsall, 2007, 233, n.65.
35. Kulikowski, 2000, 133.
36. Hyd., 63(71); Halsall, 2007, 233.
37. Hyd., 63 [71] s.a. 419, trans. Burgess, 1993, 87.
38. Heather, 2005, 265.
39. C.f. Merrills and Miles, 2014, 45.
40. C.f. Greg. Tur., 2.2.
41. See Kulikowski, 2000, 126, for dissent and bibliography, esp. n.19.
42. C.f. Merrills and Miles, 2014, 45; Astirius inflicted 'a minor defeat on the Vandals'.
43. C.f. Aug. *Ep.* 11*, where Astirius is acknowledged as leading a campaign that 'crushed' the revolt of Maximus.
44. *Chron. Gall. 452*, 29–30/89.
45. Hyd., 66(74); Philost., 12.12.
46. *Chron. Gall. 452*, 88; Olymp. frg. 33.1; Prosp., s.a. 420.
47. Olymp. frg. 33.2.
48. Emperor, *PLRE* 2, *Constantius* 17, 324; Date, Theoph. *AM* 5913; Placidia *Augusta*, Olymp. frg. 31; Prosp., s.a. 423, 425; *Chron. Gall. 452*, 29–30(88); Hydatius (67(75)) and Prosper date the elevation to 420.
49. Olymp. frg. 33.1; Valentinian *nobilissimus*, Olymp. frg. 34, Philost., 12.12.
50. Olymp. frg. 34.
51. Olymp. frg. 33.1–2; frg. 34; Philost., 12.12.
52. Philost. 12.12; Olymp. frg. 33.1–2.
53. Olymp. frg. 33.1.
54. https://www.mayoclinic.org/diseases-conditions/pleurisy/symptoms-causes/syc-20351863
55. Date, Theoph. *AM* 5913; *Chron. Gall. 452*, 29–30(88); Prosp., s.a. 421; Hyd., 68(76).
56. Theoph. *AM* 5913. Theophanes translation p.131, n.3.
57. C.f. Nixon, 2002, 72–3.

Chapter Eleven

1. Greg. Tur., 2.9.
2. Greg. Tur., 2.9.
3. The dating is slightly problematic, but unimportant. Prosper has him as *dux* in 422 (s.a. 422), but he is then acknowledged as *magister* in 423 (s.a. 423). However, Hydatius states that he is *magister* in 422 (s.a. 422).

The confusion in the sources is most likely caused by a similar political confusion following the unexpected death of Constantius III in 421. C.f. Cass. *Chron.*, s.a. 422.

4. Olymp. frg. 22.2; *PLRE 2, Boniface* 3, 238.
5. Aug. *Ep.*, 189.
6. Hydatius (70(78)) uses the phrase 'invade' when talking about Boniface retreating to Africa: see Hughes, 2012, 24–9.
7. *CAH*, 132; date, Halsall, 2007, 233; Hydatius 66(74).
8. Olymp. frg. 38, 40; Philost., 12.12.
9. O'Flynn, 1983, 74–5.
10. O'Flynn, 1983, 75.
11. Prosp., s.a. 423.
12. Olymp. frg. 38.
13. *Ann. Rav.*, s.a. 423.
14. Date, *Ann. Rav.* Col. 2. 10–12; Castinus' involvement, Prosp. s.a. 423; Hyd., s.a. 424. Matthews, 1975, 379; c.f. Soc. 7.23.
15. *Ann. Rav.* Col. 2, 10–12.
16. *PLRE 2, Castinus* 2, 270. On the theory that Theodosius accepted Castinus' own proposal of himself as candidate for consul, see O'Flynn, 1983, 75. On the failure of the embassy, see for example, Greg. Tur., 2.8; Soc., 7.23.3ff; Philost., 12.13.
17. Philost., 12.13.
18. Prosp., s.a. 424.
19. Prosp., s.a. 424.
20. Pseudo-Aug., *Ep.* 4, PL33, 1095, cited in Maenchen-Helfen, 1973, 76–7.
21. Prosp., a.424; 'John's defences were weaker because he tried to recapture Africa, over which Boniface was maintaining his control.'
22. Matthews, 1975, 379; *Sirm.* 5 (9 July 425); Arian tendencies, Freeman, 1887, 430.
23. Prosp., s.a. 424.
24. C.f. Heather, 2005, 281.
25. *Chron. Min.*, 1.470.
26. Elton, 2004, 11.
27. Prosp., s.a. 424.
28. Olymp. frg. 43. The appointment as Caesar was normal, with the appointment as *Augustus* certain to follow at the appropriate time, yet the manner of the appointment was also doubtless to ensure that Theodosius maintained seniority rather than Valentinian being seen as an equal.
29. Greg. Tur., 2.8; Olymp. frg. 46; Marcel., *com.* s.a. 424.
30. Philost., 12.13.
31. *PLRE* 2, *Candidianus* 3, 257.
32. 'With gold', Greg. Tur., 2.8.
33. For a more detailed account of the Huns, see esp. Chapter 12.
34. Philost., 12.13.

35. Philost., 12.13.
36. *CAH*, 136.
37. Olymp. frg. 43.2; Blockley, 209 and 220, n.84.
38. Philost., 12.13.
39. Soc. 7.23 suggests that the passage was assisted by angels, but a rather more prosaic manner of entry seems preferable. Philostorgius suggests that there was a battle outside the city, but his imprecise claim that 'there was some sort of battle' (12.13) may be a way of describing the confusion surrounding Aspar's unexpected entry into the city.
40. Proc., 3.3.9; Philost., 12.13.
41. Philostorgius following Olympiodorus claims 'as many as 60,000'; Olymp. frg. 43.2; Philostorgius, 12.14. Also Cass. *Chron.*, s.a. 425.
42. 'Heavy slaughter on both sides', Olymp. frg. 43.2.
43. Philost., 12.14; Greg. Tur., 2.8; Prosp., s.a. 425.
44. Philost., 12.14 (Olymp. frg. 43.2). On the ceding of Pannonia, see Maenchen-Helfen, 1973, 89.
45. O'Flynn, 1983, 74.
46. Hyd., s.a. 425; *PLRE* 2, Fl. *Constantius Felix* 14, 461. O'Flynn follows Prosper in dating the patricianship to 429 (Prosp., s.a. 429).
47. *Chron. Min.*, 1.471.
48. It is possible that either luck or his political and marital contacts helped Castinus to survive at this time, although without evidence it has been decided that the main reason was his decision to maintain a low profile.
49. *Cod. Th.*, 6.2.25 (26 April 426).
50. Muhlberger, 2006, 33–4.
51. See e.g. Hughes, 2010, 2012.
52. For a detailed account of Gaiseric's life, see Hughes, 2017, *passim*.

Select Bibliography

Primary Sources:

Additamenta ad Chronicon Prosperi Hauniensis, Chronica Minora, Vol. 1: The Copenhagen Continuation of Prosper: A Translation, Muhlberger, S., *Florilegium*, Vol. 6 (1984), pp.71–95.

Ammianus Marcellinus, *The Histories*, trans. Rolfe, J.C. (Harvard, 1986)

Anglo Saxon Chronicle: https://www.gutenberg.org/cache/epub/657/pg657.html

Annals of Ravenna, Bischoff, Bernhard and Koehler, Wilhelm, '*Eine illustrierte Aus gabe der spätantiken Ravennater Annalen*', *Medieval Studies in Memory of A. Kingsley Porter*, Vol. 1 (Cambridge Mass., 1939), pp.125–138; text at pp.127–129, 131.

Augustine, St, *Epistles*: http://www.newadvent.org/fathers/1102.htm: http://www. ccel.org/ccel/schaff/npnf101.i.html: https://ia601408.us.archive.org/14/items/ lettersofstaugus00sparuoft/lettersofstaugus00sparuoft.pdf

Cassiodorus, *Chronica*: http://ia311003.us.archive.org/0/items/chronicaminorasa 11momm/chronicaminorasa11momm.pdf

Claudian, Platnauer, M. (trans.), *The Complete Works* (Harvard, 1922). http:// penelope.uchicago.edu/Thayer/E/Roman/Texts/Claudian/home.html

Codex Justinianus: The Code of Justinian, trans. Blume, F.H. http://uwacadweb. uwyo.edu/blume&justinian/default.asp

Codex Theodosianus: The Theodosian Code and Novels and the Sirmondian Constitutions, Pharr, C., Davidson, T.S. and Pharr, M.B. (Princeton, 1952)

Consularia Constantinopolitana, Burgess, R.W., *The Chronicle of Hydatius and the Consularia Constantinopolitana: Two Contemporary Accounts of the Final Years of the Roman Empire* (Oxford, 1993)

Epistulae Austrasicae (Austrasian Letters): http://www.dmgh.de/de/fs1/object/ display/bsb00000534_00117.html?zoom=0.75&sortIndex= 040:010:0003:010:00:00, especially http://www.dmgh.de/de/fs1/object/display/ bsb00000534_00142.html?sortIndex=040%3A010%3A0003%3A010% 3A00%3A00&zoom=0.75

Fredegar: https://www.dmgh.de/mgh_ss_rer_merov_2/index.htm#page/(III)/ mode/1up, especially https://www.dmgh.de/mgh_ss_rer_merov_2/index. htm#page/71/mode/1up

Gallic Chronicle of 452 in Murray, A.C., *From Roman to Merovingian Gaul* (Ontario, 2000)

Gerontius, *Vita Melania*, Clark, E.A. (ed., trans.) *The Life of Melania the Younger* (London, 1984)

Gildas, 'The Text of Gildas: *de Excidio et Conquestu Britanniae*' (Parts 1 and 2, Chapters 1–37): http://www.vortigernstudies.org.uk/arthist/vortigern quotesgil.htm

Gregory of Tours: https://sourcebooks.fordham.edu/basis/gregory-hist.asp

Hieronymus: *see* Jerome

Hydatius, Burgess, R.W., *The Chronicle of Hydatius and the Consularia Constantinopolitana: Two Contemporary Accounts of the Final Years of the Roman Empire* (Oxford, 1993)

Innocent, *Epistles*: https://www.documentacatholicaomnia.eu/01_01_0401-0417-_Innocentius_I,_Sanctus.html

Isidore of Seville, *Chronicon*, trans. Wolf, K.B. http://www.ccel.org/ccel/pearse/morefathers/files/isidore_chronicon_01_trans.htm

Isidore of Seville, *Historia de Regibus Gothorum, Wandalorum et Suevorum* http://e-spania.revues.org/15552#tocto1n5
http://www.thelatinlibrary.com/isidore/historia.shtml

Jerome, *Apologeticum adversus Rufinum*: http://www.newadvent.org/fathers/27103.htm

Jerome, *Epistles*: http://www.newadvent.org/fathers/3001.htm

Jordanes, trans. Mierow, C.C. (1908), *The Origin and Deeds of the Goths* (Princeton, reprint, 2006, Lenox, M.A.)

Jordanes, *Getica (The Origins and Deeds of the Goths)*, trans. Mierow, C.C.
http://www.northvegr.org/lore/jgoth/index.php (February 2010)
http://people.ucalgary.ca/~vandersp/Courses/texts/jordgeti.html (February 2010)

Jordanes, *Romana (De summa temporum vel origine actibusque gentis Romanorum)*: selected text and translation: http://www.harbornet.com/folks/theedrich/Goths/Romana.htm
http://www.thelatinlibrary.com/iordanes.html

Maier, I.G., *Latin Imperial Laws and Letters (AD 306–565) not included in the Codes and Novels of Theodosius and Iustinianus* (Internet Publishing, Melbourne, 2012) www.notitiadignitatum.org/extracod.pdf

Marcellinus *comes*: http://www.documentacatholicaomnia.eu/02m/0474-0534,_Marcellinus_Comes,_Chronicum,_MLT.pdf; Croke, B., *The Chronicle of Marcellinus: A Translation and Commentary* (Sydney, 1995)

Merobaudes, *Flavius Merobaudes: A Translation and Historical Commentary*, Clover, F.M. (Philadelphia, 1971)

Michael the Syrian: https://archive.org/details/ChronicleOfMichaelTheGreat PatriarchOfTheSyrians

Notitia Dignitatum: https://archive.org/details/notitiadignitat00seecgoog/page/n5

Olympiodorus: Blockley, R.C., *The Fragmentary Classicizing Historians of the Later Roman Empire II: Eunapius, Olympiodorus, Priscus and Malchus* (Francis Cairns, 1983)

Orosius: Deferrari, R.J. (trans.), *The Fathers of the Church: Paulus Orosius, The Seven Books of History Against the Pagans* (Washington D.C., 1964)

Panegyrici Latini: In Praise of Later Roman Emperors, trans. Nixon, C.E.V. and Rodgers, B.S. (UCP, 1994)

Paulinus of Pella: https://penelope.uchicago.edu/Thayer/E/Roman/Texts/Paulinus_Pellaeus/home.html

Philostorgius: Amidon, P.R., *Philostorgius: Church History* (Atlanta, 2007)

Possidius, *Vita Augustini*: http://www.tertullian.org/fathers/possidius_life_of_augustine_02_text.htm

Priscus, in Blockley, R.C., *The Fragmentary Classicizing Historians of the Later Roman Empire*, Vol. 2 (Liverpool, 1983), pp.222–379.

Priscus, *Testimonia*, in Blockley, R.C., *The Fragmentary Classicizing Historians of the Later Roman Empire*, Vol. 2 (Liverpool, 1983), pp.222–400.

Procopius, *The Vandalic War*: https://www.gutenberg.org/ebooks/16765

Prosper Tiro, *Chronicum*: http://www.documentacatholicaomnia.eu/02m/0390_0463,_Prosperus_Aquitanus,_Chronicum_Integrum_In_Dua_Partes_Distributum,_MLT.pdf

Prosper Tiro, *Chronicum*, trans. Murray, A.C., *From Roman to Merovingian Gaul: A Reader* (Ontario, 2000)

Querolus: https://archive.org/details/aululariasiveque00peipuoft

Rutilius Namatianus, *de Reditu suo*, 41f: http://penelope.uchicago.edu/Thayer/E/Roman/Texts/Rutilius_Namatianus/text*.html (July 2009)

Sidonius Apollinaris, *Carmina*: http://www.documentacatholicaomnia.eu/02m/0430-0489,_Sidonius_Apollinaris_Episcopus,_Carmina,_MLT.pdf

Sidonius Apollinaris, *Letters*: http://www.tertullian.org/fathers/#sidonius_apollinaris

Sidonius Apollinaris, *Poems and Letters* (2 vols), trans. Anderson, W.B. (Harvard, 1936/1965)

Socrates Scholasticus, *Ecclesiastical History*: http://www.newadvent.org/fathers/2601.htm

Sozomen, *Ecclesiastical History*: http://www.hourofthetime.com/1_LF/November2012/Hour_Of_The_Time_11042012-The_Ecclesiastical_History_Of_Sozomen_And_Philostorgius-1855.pdf

The Visigothic Code: https://libro.uca.edu/vcode/visigoths.htm

Theophanes, *The Chronicle of Theophanes Confessor: Byzantine and Near Eastern History AD 284–813*, Mango, C. and Scott, R. (trans.) (Oxford, 1997)

Theophanes, *Chronographia*, trans. Niebuhr, B.G. (Bonn, 1849) http://www.veritatis-societas.org/203_CSHB/0700-0800,_Theophanes_Abbas_Confessor_Chronographia_%28CSHB_Classeni_Recensio%29,_GR.pdf (April 2010)

Zonaras, *Epitome Historiarum*: http://www.documentacatholicaomnia.eu/30_20_1050-1150-_Ioannes_Zonaras.html (Greek)

Zosimus, *New History*, trans. Ridley, R.T. (Canberra, 1982)

Secondary Sources

Afanasyev, I., Dresvina, J. and Kooper, E. (eds), *The Medieval Chronicle X* (Leiden, 2015)

Amidon, P.R., *Philostorgius: Church History* (Society of Biblical Literature, 2007)

Blockley, R.C., *The Fragmentary Classicizing of Historians of the Later Roman Empire*, Vol. 2 (Liverpool, 1983)

Brown, P.R.L., 'Aspects of the Christianization of the Roman Aristocracy' in *Journal of Roman Studies*, Vol. 51 (Issue 1–2, 1961), pp.1–11.

Burns, T.S., *Rome and the Barbarians, 100 BC–AD 400* (Baltimore, 2003)

Burns, T.S., *Barbarians Within the Gates of Rome* (Indiana, 1994)

Bury, J.B., *A History of the Later Roman Empire*, 2 Vols. (London, 1923) http://penelope.uchicago.edu/Thayer/E/Roman/Texts/secondary/BURLAT

Cambridge Ancient History: see Cameron, A. and Garnsey, P.

Cameron, A. and Garnsey, P. (eds), *The Cambridge Ancient History, Volume XIII: The Late Empire A.D. 337–425* (Cambridge, 2004)

Cameron, A., *Claudian: Poetry and Propaganda at the Court of Honorius* (Oxford, 1970)

Collins, R., *Visigothic Spain 409–711* (Oxford, 2006)

Costa, D., *The Lost Gold of Rome: The Hunt for Alaric's Treasure* (Stroud, 2007)

Diaz, P.C., 'Visigothic Political Institutions' in Heather, P. (ed.), *The Visigoths From the Migration Period to the Seventh Century: An Ethnographic Perspective* (San Marino, 1999), pp.321–372.

Drinkwater, J.F., *The Alamanni and Rome: 213–496* (Oxford, 2007)

Drinkwater, J.F. and Elton, H. (eds), *Fifth-Century Gaul: A Crisis of Identity?* (Cambridge, 2002)

Dunn, G.D., 'Flavius Constantius, Galla Placidia and the Aquitanian Settlement of the Goths', *Phoenix LXIX Nos. 3–4* (Fall-winter 2015), pp.376–393.

Dunn, G.D., '*Quid Habuerit Antiqua Consuetudo*: Zosimus of Rome and Hilary of Narbonne' in *Revue d'Histoire Ecclésiastique* (Vol. 110, 2015), pp.1–2, 31–56.

Dunn, G.D., 'Flavius Constantius and Affairs in Gaul between 411 and 417' in *Journal of the Australian Early Medieval Association*, Vol. 10 (2014), pp.1–21.

Dunn, G.D., 'Innocent I, Alaric and Honorius: Church and State in Early Fifth-Century Rome' in Luckensmeyer, D. and Allen, P., *Studies of Religion and Politics in the Early Christian Centuries* (Strathfield, NSW, 2010), pp.243–62.

Dunn, G.D., 'The Care of the Poor in Rome and Alaric's Sieges' in *Prayer and Spirituality in the Early Church, Vol. 5: Poverty and Riches*, eds Dunn, G.D., Luckensmeyer, D. and Cross, L. (Strathfield, NSW, 2009), pp.319–336.

Dzino, D. and Parry, K. (eds), *Byzantium, its Neighbours and its Cultures (Byzantina Australiensia 20)* (Brisbane, 2014)

Elton, H., *Warfare in Roman Europe: A.D. 350–425* (Oxford, 2004)

Elton, H., *Constantine III, DIR*: http://www.roman-emperors.org/westemp5.htm#Note (1999)

Fabbro, E., '"*Capitur Urbs Quae totum Cepit Orbem*": The Fates of the Sack of Rome (410) in Early Medieval Historiography' in *The Medieval Chronicle X*, Afanasyev, I., Dresvina, J. and Kooper, E. (eds), (Leiden, 2015), pp.49–68.

Fossier, R. (ed.), *The Cambridge Illustrated History of the Middle Ages 350–950* (Cambridge, 1989)

Freeman, E.A., 'Aetius and Boniface' in *The English Historical Review*, Vol. 2, No. 7 (July 1887), pp.417–465.

Garnica, A.M.J., 'Settlement of the Visigoths in the Fifth Century' in Heather, P. (ed.), *The Visigoths From the Migration Period to the Seventh Century: An Ethnographic Perspective* (San Marino, 1999), pp.93–128.

Gelens, T., 'The Sack of Rome: A Symbol of Change; The Sack of Rome of 410 AD in Contemporary and Near-Contemporary Sources', MA Dissertation (Nijmegen, 2014)

Goffart, W., *Barbarians and Romans, A.D. 418–584: The Techniques of Accommodation* (Princeton University Press, 1980)

Goldsworthy, A., *The Fall of the West: The Death of the Roman Superpower* (London, 2009)

Halsall, G., *Barbarian Migrations and the Roman West: 376–568* (Cambridge, 2007)

Harvey, P.B. Jr. and Conybeare, C. (eds), *Maxima Debetur Magistro Reverentia: Essays on Rome and the Roman Tradition in Honor of Russell T. Scott* (Biblioteca 01, Athenaeum 56) (Como, 2009)

Heather, P., *The Fall of the Roman Empire* (Macmillan, 2005)

Heather, P. (ed.), *The Visigoths From the Migration Period to the Seventh Century: An Ethnographic Perspective* (San Marino, 1999)

Heather, P., *Goths and Romans: 332–489* (Oxford, 1994)

Heather, P., *Goths and Romans: 332–489* (Oxford, 1991)

Hodgkin, T., *Italy and her Invaders: Volume 2: Book 2, The Hunnish Invasions; Book 3, The Vandal Invasion and the Herulian Mutiny* (Oxford, 1892)

Hughes, I., *Attila the Hun: Arch-Enemy of Rome* (Barnsley, 2019)

Hughes, I., *Gaiseric: The Vandal Who Sacked Rome* (Barnsley, 2017)

Hughes, I., *Aetius: Attila's Nemesis* (Barnsley, 2012)

Hughes, I., *Stilicho: The Vandal Who Saved Rome* (Barnsley, 2010)

Jones, A.H.M., *The Decline of the Ancient World* (London, 1990)

Jones, A.H.M., *The Later Roman Empire 284–602: A Social and Administrative Survey*, 2 Volumes (Oxford, 1973)

Kelly, C., *Attila The Hun: Barbarian Terror and the Fall of the Roman Empire* (Bodley Head, 2008)

Kulikowski, M., *Rome's Gothic Wars* (New York, 2007)

Kulikowski, M., 'The Visigothic Settlement in Aquitania: The Imperial Perspective' in Mathisen, R.W. and Shanzer, D. (eds), *Society and Culture in Late Antique Gaul: Revisiting the Sources* (Aldershot, 2001), pp.26–38.

Kulikowski, M., 'Barbarians in Gaul, Usurpers in Britain' in *Britannia* 31 (2000), pp.325–45.

Kulikowski, M., 'The Career of the *Comes Hispaniarum* Asterius' in *Phoenix*, Vol. 54, Nos. 1/2 (Spring-summer 2000), pp.123–141.

Laisathit, P., 'Ravenna's Attempts to Save Rome from the 410 Sack': https://www.academia.edu/33233720/Ravennas_attempts_to_save_Rome_from_the_410_sack

Latham-Sprinkle, J., '"For Assur Comes with Them": Reassessing the Alan Presence in Hispania, 409–418' (UCD History 17, forthcoming) (adapted version of paper given at IMBAS 2012): https://www.academia.edu/3884365/For_Assur_Comes_with_Them_Reassessing_the_Alan_Presence_in_Hispania_409_418

Liebeschuetz, J.H.G.W., 'Citizen Status and Law in the Roman Empire and the Visigothic Kingdom' in W. Pohl and H. Reimitz (eds.), *Strategies of Distinction: The Construction of Ethnic Communities, 300–800* (Leiden, 1998), pp.131–152.

Liebeschuetz, J.H.W.G., *Barbarians and Bishops: Army, Church and State in the Age of Arcadius and Chrysostom* (Clarendon Press, 1992)

Lipps, J., Machado, C. and von Rummel, P. (eds), *Palilia 28; The Sack of Rome in 410 AD: The Event, Its Context and its Impact* (Wiesbaden, 2013)

López-Quiroga, J. and Martínez Tejera, A.M. (coord.), *In Tempore Sueborum: The Time of the Sueves in Gallaecia (411–585), The First Medieval Kingdom of the West* (Exhibition Catalogue, Ourense, 2017)

Luckensmeyer, D. and Allen, P., *Studies of Religion and Politics in the Early Christian Centuries* (Strathfield, NSW, 2010)

McEvoy, M., 'Between the Old Rome and the New: Imperial Co-operation ca. 400–500 CE' in Dzino, D. and Parry, K. (eds), *Byzantium, its Neighbours and its Cultures* (Byzantina Australiensia 20) (Brisbane, 2014), pp.245–268.

McEvoy, M., 'Rome and the Transformation of the Imperial Office in the Late Fourth/Mid-Fifth Centuries AD' in *Papers of the British School at Rome*, Vol. 78 (2010), pp.151–192.

Maenchen-Helfen, O.J., *The World of the Huns: Studies in Their History and Culture* (University of California Press, 1973)

Maier, I.G., *Latin Imperial Laws and Letters (AD 306–565) not included in the Codes and Novels of Theodosius and Iustinianus* (Internet Publishing, Melbourne, 2012) www.notitiadignitatum.org/extracod.pdf

Martindale, J.R., *The Prosopography of the Later Roman Empire, Volume II: A.D. 395–527* (Cambridge, 1980)

Mathisen, R.W., '*Roma a Gothis Alarico duce capta est*: Ancient Accounts of the Sack of Rome in 410 CE', Lipps, J., Machado, C. and von Rummel, P. (eds), *Palilia 28: The Sack of Rome in 410 AD: The Event, Its Context and its Impact* (Wiesbaden, 2013), pp.87–102.

Mathisen, R.W. and Shanzer, D. (eds), *Romans, Barbarians and the Transformation of the Roman World* (Farnham, 2011)

Mathisen, R.W. and Shanzer, D. (eds), *Society and Culture in Late Antique Gaul: Revisiting the Sources* (Aldershot, 2001)

Mathisen, R.W., *Roman Aristocrats in Barbarian Gaul: Strategies for Survival in an Age of Transition* (University of Texas, 1993)

Matthews, J., *Western Aristocracies and Imperial Court A.D. 364–425* (Oxford, 1998)

Matthews, J.F., 'The Letters of Symmachus' in Binns, J.W. (ed.), *Latin Literature of the Fourth Century* (London, 1975)

Merrills, A. and Miles, R., *The Vandals* (Malden, 2010)

Mitchell, S., *A History of the Later Roman Empire, A.D. 284–641* (Oxford, 2009)

Morris, J., *The Age of Arthur: A History of the British Isles from 350–650* (London, 2001)

Muhlberger, S., *The Fifth-Century Chroniclers: Prosper, Hydatius and the Gallic Chronicle of 452: Prosper, Hydatius and the Gallic Chronicler of 452* (Francis Cairns, 2006)

Murray, A.C., *From Roman to Merovingian Gaul* (Ontario, 2000)

Nixon, C.E.V., 'Relations between Visigoths and Romans in Fifth-Century Gaul' in Drinkwater, J.F. and Elton, H. (eds.), *Fifth-Century Gaul: A Crisis of Identity?* (Cambridge, 2002), pp.64–74.

Norwich, J.J., *Byzantium: The Early Centuries* (Viking, 1988)

O'Flynn, J., *Generalissimos of the Western Roman Empire* (University of Alberta Press, 1981)

Oost, S.I., 'Aëtius and Majorian' in *Classical Philology*, Vol. 59, No. 1 (January 1964), pp.23–29.

Papadopoulos, I., 'The Enemy Within: The Rise and Influence of Conspiracy Theories in Rome before the Gothic sack (410 AD)', *Leeds International Medieval Congress* (2017) https://www.academia.edu/33704605/The_Enemy_Within_The_Rise_and_Influence_of_Conspiracy_Theories_in_Rome_before_the_Gothic_sack_410_AD

Pawluk, M., 'Theodosius, a son of Athaulf and Galla Placidia', *Eos*, XCII (2005), pp.224–243.

The Prosopography of the Later Roman Empire: see Martindale, 1980

Ribeiro Machado, C.A., 'The Roman Aristocracy and the Imperial Court, before and after the Sack' in Lipps, J., Machado, C. and von Rummel, P. (eds), *Palilia 28: The Sack of Rome in 410 AD: The Event, Its Context and its Impact* (Wiesbaden, 2014), pp.49–76.

Ribeiro Machado, C.A., 'The Roman Aristocracy and the Imperial Court, before and after the Sack' in Machado, C., von Rummel, P. and Lipps, J. (eds), *The Sack of Rome in 410 A.D.* (Palilia) (Wiesbaden, 2013)

Ridley, R.T. (trans.), *Zosimus: New History* (Sidney, 1982)

Roymans, N., 'Gold, Germanic *foederati* and the end of imperial power in the Late Roman North' in Roymans, N., Heeren, S. and De Clercq, W., *Social Dynamics in the North-West Frontiers of the Late Roman Empire: Beyond decline or transformation* (Amsterdam, 2017), pp.57–80.

Salzman, M.R., 'Memory and Meaning: Pagans and 410' in Lipps, J., Machado, C. and von Rummel, P. (eds), *The Sack of Rome in 410 AD: The Event, its Context and its Impact: Proceedings of the Conference Held at the German Archaeological Institute at Rome, 04–06 November 2010* (Wiesbaden, 2013), pp.215–310.

Salzman, M.R., 'Apocalypse Then? Jerome and the Fall of Rome in 410 CE' in Harvey, P.B. Jr. and Conybeare, C. (eds), *Maxima Debetur Magistro Reverentia: Essays on Rome and the Roman Tradition in Honor of Russell T. Scott* (Biblioteca 01, Athenaeum 56) (Como, 2009), pp.175–192.

Schwarcz, A., 'Visigothic Settlement, *Hospitalitas* and Army Payment Reconsidered' in Mathisen, R.W. and Shanzer, D., *Romans, Barbarians and the Transformation of the Roman World* (Farnham, 2011), pp.265–270.

Thompson, E.A., *Romans and Barbarians: The Decline of the Western Empire* (Wisconsin, 1982)

Thompson, E.A., 'Peasant Revolts in Late Roman Gaul and Spain', *Past & Present*, No. 2 (November 1952), pp.11–23.

Ward-Perkins, B., *The Fall of Rome and the End of Civilization* (Oxford, 2006)

Wijnendaele, J.W.P., *Heraclianus* (2020) http://www.roman-emperors.org/HeraclianusComAfr.htm#_ftnref9

Wijnendaele, J.W.P., 'Sarus the Goth: From Imperial Commander to Warlord', *Early Medieval Europe* 27 (4) (2019), pp.469–493.

Wijnendaele, J.W.P., 'The Manufacture of Heraclianus' Usurpation (413 C.E.)', *Phoenix: The Journal of the Classical Association of Canada* 71 (1–2) (2017), pp.138–156.

Williams, S. and Friell, G., *Theodosius: The Empire at Bay* (London, 1994)

Wolfram, H., *History of the Goths* (California, 1990)

Woods, D., 'On the Alleged Letters of Honorius to the Cities of Britain in 410', *Latomus* 71 (2012), pp.818–826.

Index